My Daddy's Going Away ...

Helping families cope with paternal separation

Christopher MacGregor

Giddy Mangoes Limited

© Christopher MacGregor 2009
My Daddy's Going Away ...
ISBN 978-0-9564651-0-8

Published by **Giddy Mangoes Limited**
14 Gableson Avenue, Brighton, East Sussex, BN1 5FG

Concept, design, words and website: Chris MacGregor

Original artwork: Sami-Jo Cook-Wild and Lindsey Emma Walker

Final illustrations: Jerry Pyke

HRH The Prince of Wales photograph by kind permission of Mario Testino

Book typeset by Michael Walsh at THE BETTER BOOK COMPANY
5 Lime Close, Chichester PO19 6SW

and printed by
ASHFORD COLOUR PRESS
Unit 600 Fareham Reach
Fareham Road
Gosport Hants PO13 0FW

Visit **www.mydaddysgoingaway.com** for ideas, support and fun things to do.

For Ben and Ellie, with love from Daddy

I am delighted to introduce this charming book; it not only supports two charities with which I am closely involved, Combat Stress and my Foundation for Integrated Health, but thoughtfully prepares young children and their families to cope with the challenges of temporary paternal separation. As a father, I can only too well understand the strains on family wellbeing that absence can bring. Within this book, each cheerful illustration complements an insightful verse that, on many levels, can be used within your community or family to strengthen bonds and develop coping strategies. 'My Daddy's Going Away ...' should really be read by all families.

My Daddy's Going Away ...

Christopher MacGregor

My Daddy's going away you know
Mummy says it's for a while
We'll miss our hugs and story-time
And certainly his smile.

Dad says he won't be gone too long
But only time will tell
How long it takes in far off lands
For his socks to really smell.

He'll fly upon an aeroplane

Magic carpet of the skies

Leading those who follow him

To win the hard fought prize.

Together they will conquer all
That comes into their path...
'Though I wish he was at home with me
Putting bubbles in my bath!

My Daddy's still away you know
Mummy says he's working hard
We chatter on the telephone
And I've sent a Birthday card.

From time to time Dad sends us stuff
And that is really cool
But best of all I like it when
We can show things off at school.

I know he loves me more each day
Our separation grows
It's hard enough to squeeze it all
Between my head and toes.

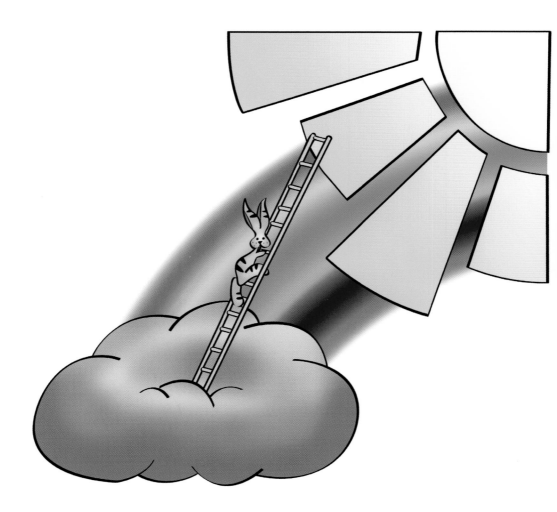

If the sun gives way to cloud
And I'm not sure why he's gone
I'll talk to Mum and my best friend
And that will make me strong.

We miss each other most of all
As we snuggle in our beds
But we share the same warm blanket
Of stars above our heads.

Every night before he goes to sleep
Daddy says a little prayer
Sometimes I think I hear it come
And whisper in the air.

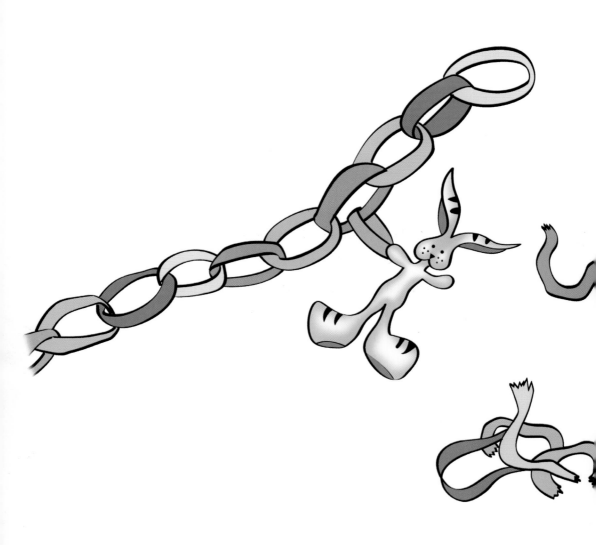

To mark the passing of the time
We'll colour in a chart
Paint calendars and paper-chains
And call it 'funky art'.

When Dad comes home we'll go on trips
Fly kites and camping too
Explore the world of dinosaurs
And see tigers at the zoo.

My Daddy's coming home you know
The excitement makes me quake
We'll hang balloons and jump up high
And make a chocolate cake!

My Daddy's coming home today

I can't believe it's true

A hug is worth a thousand words...

...My kiss just, "I love you".

They fight our wars. We fight their battles.

The Prince's Foundation for
Integrated Health

A significant minority of the men and women returning from combat suffer from Post Traumatic Stress Disorder (PTSD) or have other psychological illnesses that may include: anxiety, phobic disorders, social dysfunction, problems with anger, alcohol misuse, illicit drug abuse and addiction. These symptoms affect veterans, their families, friends and the communities in which they live.

Combat Stress is the lead charity tackling this issue and it does this by providing evidence-based therapy through:

1. Three short stay residential treatment centres across the UK.

2. A Community Outreach Service delivering treatment, care and support to Veterans and their families at home.

For more information please visit
www.combatstress.org.uk

The Prince's Foundation for Integrated Heal works to ensure integrated healthcare available for everyone. That means bringi together medicine with prevention, mi with body, complementary with mainstrea to reach the roots of illness. We think th patients should be treated as whole hum beings – with bodies, minds and spirit and understand that whatever affects o part affects all three. Secondly, it is abc integrating complementary treatments, whi have evidence of clinical effectiveness w conventional healthcare, if in the patien best interests. It is clinically led by a group Fellows – scientists and practising docto nurses, and other healthcare professiona some are also researchers and practition of complementary medicine. The Foundati is a registered Charity and has no financial vested interests in any products or services.

For more information please visit
www.fihealth.org.uk

For a great explorer and much missed friend:
Louise Cummings

CASE #41029973876628

Case Holder Notes:

TUESDAY – 7.21 a.m.

Primary Subject wakes.
 Energy Tension high.

TUESDAY

7.28 a.m.

Mum was moving around in our living room, which also happens to be our kitchen, and that was what had woken me up.

Mum's the Ultimate Early Bird. That's what Auntie Dodo calls her. Granny used to be the Early Bird, but Mum's the Ultimate. Sometimes when I wake up early like today and hear her through the walls, I imagine that she has, in fact, turned into a bird. A small brown one with a dash of yellow for a beak. A sparrow perhaps, or a robin, darting here and there, always busy, busy, busy and on the go. It's not difficult to picture Mum like that.

Recently, she's been revising for something at work. The last few mornings she's been getting up even earlier than usual, and I've found her poring over the pile of heavy books that now lives in the middle of our dining table.

Though I'd been awake for a while, I hadn't made any move to get up. I'd pulled the duvet right up so it came over my head and no part of my body was exposed. I'm tall for my age, the tallest in my class, in fact, and so I had to wrap the duvet around me very carefully and then tuck my head down so even my curly black hair was covered. It felt so warm and safe in there, all wrapped up like that. I could pretend that I wasn't really in my bedroom at all, but in a completely different place; far away from South London, far away from my life and far away from what had happened yesterday.

But then a memory started to play in my head and I felt a heavy ball growing in the pit of my stomach. It was a lot of feelings all mixed up together: worry, anger, embarrassment and sadness – I couldn't even name everything that was swirling around in there. All I knew was that it hurt.

'A-na! Are you up yet?' Mum called through my door.

I lay very still.

'Ana?' Mum's voice went up a pitch.

Maybe I could pretend I wasn't feeling well.

My hand went to my throat. It suddenly felt sore, as though I'd made it happen just by thinking about it. Then I put my other hand on my stomach, which still felt as if it was churning. I couldn't push away the memory of what had happened the day before, no matter how hard I tried. I closed my eyes tightly, even more sure now that I did have a sore throat.

The door of my bedroom squeaked open, and I heard Mum give the smallest of sighs when she saw I was still buried beneath my duvet, unmoving.

'Are you okay under there, poppet?' She took a couple of steps towards me.

I didn't make a move. Instead, I mumbled into my pillow, 'I'm not feeling well.'

I didn't think that she'd heard what I'd said, but then my mattress creaked and I felt it shift as Mum sat down next to me.

'What's up?' she asked gently.

3

'My throat's sore. I don't think … I don't think I feel well enough to go to school.'

'Okay,' I heard her say.

'Really?' I said, unable to hide the relief from my voice. Mum had believed me so easily.

'Let's look at you, pops.' She pulled the duvet down gently so my head was just peeping out. 'There you are.' She pressed her palm against my forehead. 'Hmm. Better do a full examination.'

Mum's a nurse at the local hospital. My granny, who passed away a couple of years ago, used to say that Mum could have been a doctor. 'And she still can be, if she wants to!' my Auntie Dodo would say back in a flash each time.

Susie from my class at school once told me that she's never been able to fake being unwell – her mum's a nurse too and can tell when she's making it up. But my mum always takes me seriously.

It made me feel even worse that I was lying to her, but I knew it might work and I wouldn't have to go in. A couple of weeks ago when something else had happened that made me want to hide away, Mum had believed me when I told her I felt like I was going to be sick and she stayed at home with me. We watched telly together and she made me plates of dry toast. I didn't like doing it, but I really didn't want to go to school that day.

'Can I look down your throat?' Mum asked me. 'Open up as wide as you can. Go "aaaah".'

Guilt formed inside me as I looked into her worried eyes. The soreness I thought I'd felt just moments ago had vanished completely. But I did as I was told, and Mum peered into my mouth.

'It doesn't look red,' she said. 'But let me check your temperature.'

After the thermometer told us there was nothing wrong, Mum checked me all over once more and then she gave me a look that I understood straight away.

'I still have to go to school,' I said for her.

'If you start to feel worse then tell your teacher, okay? I'll collect you if you need to come home.' She reached for me, cupping my cheek in her hand, which felt cool and soft against my skin, like a wave-worn seashell. 'Is there anything you want to talk about?' she asked.

I shook my head and fiddled with a bit of the duvet that was bunched up around me. The words were in my mouth. I could tell her, but something was stopping me. I suddenly felt so lonely that I thought I might start crying. It's an odd kind of loneliness when you're with someone you love but you can't tell them how you're really feeling.

Mum looked like she wanted to say something else too, but then she bit her lip and went quiet for a few moments. 'How about I make us something nice for breakfast?' She searched my face for an answer, but I kept looking down at my hands. 'And remember, Dodo's coming over tonight – it's Chewy Tuesday.'

We've been having Chewy Tuesdays for a long time – me, Mum and Auntie Dodo. It's not a good name but somehow it's stuck. Chewy Tuesdays came from a night when Dodo cooked for us. She made us brownies that turned out so chewy they'd almost glued our jaws together. Now we take it in turns to cook for each other every Tuesday, but we don't let Dodo make brownies (although she keeps threatening that one day she'll try again).

Remembering Dodo's hopeful face as we chewed and chewed on those brownies made me smile. We've always been close – I was actually the one who gave her that nickname. I couldn't say Dolores properly when I was little, so I called her Dodo instead. Now Mum calls her that too, or Doe for short.

'There's a smile,' Mum said. 'I saw it!' She pulled me in for a hug and I wrapped my arms around her. It made me feel a bit better to hold her. And I felt my heart lighten a little at the thought of seeing Dodo. Maybe I could talk to her about what had been happening.

TUESDAY

8.08 a.m.

Mum slid another pancake onto my plate.

'I'm full up.' I motioned, pushing the plate away from me. It bumped against Mum's pile of books that were stacked up on the table.

'Are you sure you don't want another? You've only had half of one.'

'No, I'm okay,' I said, trying not to meet her eyes. Knowing that I was going to school had taken away my appetite.

'All right,' Mum said, but she didn't take my plate away. She looked at me in a way that made me feel like there were beams reaching out to me from her eyes. 'How's your throat feeling now?'

'Not too bad,' I lied, then changed the subject. 'I guess I'd better get ready to leave.'

'I'll walk with you today,' Mum said quickly.

'Don't worry, I'm going to walk with Layla. She stayed with her dad last night so we're going to meet at the corner of the road.'

Layla's my best friend. She spends part of the week with her mum and the rest with her dad. He owns a bike shop on our road, and when she stays with him, we always walk to school together.

'Okay, but I think I'd better have a word with your teacher to let her know you weren't feeling well this morning – just in case you get worse.' Once again, I felt guilt seep through me.

'I'm fine now,' I said, standing, although I could feel my stomach flipping at the thought of returning to school.

'Really?' Mum asked as she walked over to me. I'm almost as tall as her so she looked me right in the eye as she said this.

I must get my height and build from my dad, although I don't know who he is as I've never met him. Mum told me that she was very young when she had me, and that my dad moved away before she could tell him about me. Once I asked her whether we might be able to find him, but that was when Granny was alive and she overheard and got cross, saying we didn't need to be going down *that* path. Luckily, my mum does the job of two parents and she's pretty great at it.

I looked back at mum's kind eyes locking onto mine and wished I'd never said anything in the first place. She placed her hand gently on my forehead again. 'Still no temperature. I think you're okay, but see how you go. You'd better leave soon if you're meeting Layla.'

I had to force myself to complete all the things that I needed to do before I left: brush teeth, find bag, put on coat. Then I tied up my dark, unruly curls in a loose ponytail.

'Don't forget your hat and scarf, Ana. It looks cold out there,' Mum said when I was at the door.

She placed the hat securely on my head and wrapped the scarf round my neck several times. I felt all warm and bundled up, but I slumped at the thought of having to leave.

Mum tipped my chin up so she could look at me properly. 'There's my girl.' She smiled. 'Have a good day, and if you feel any worse, tell your teacher and I'll come to get you,' she said.

When I finally made it out of the door, our next-door neighbour's front door opened too. Sami scampered out into the corridor – he's one of the kids that lives there, but he was nothing but a blur of school uniform and legs this morning. Sami runs everywhere. Behind him, I saw his mum, Benny, trying to manoeuvre a pram out of the door. Her other children trailed behind her: Denise, Rita (who's Sami's twin) and Tio.

I remember the day when Rita and Sami came home from the hospital and Tio and I were allowed to hold them very, very carefully. Now it felt like a long time since we'd sat next to each other on the sofa, holding the tiny twins.

'Sami, come back!' Benny yelled.

Mum had followed me out into the corridor and turned to Benny. 'Benny! I was hoping I'd catch you.'

'Hi, Lettie.' Benny grinned.

Mum leaned over the pram to look at tiny, sleeping Mario and then started to talk about baby stuff with Benny. I kept my gaze fixed on the ground. I wanted to keep walking, but I knew it would seem weird if I did. And Mum would be sure to call me back. I could only see my shoes from this angle, but if I raised my head a little, then I could just about make out the shadows of Denise, Rita and Tio in front of me.

We've lived next door to each other for ever. Denise is the eldest at thirteen, there are only a few months between Tio and me (he turned eleven before me) and Sami and Rita are five years old.

I used to think of Tio as a coiled spring, leaping into action at a second's notice. He's a bit like Sami in that sense, always moving, scuffing his feet against the pavement if we're standing in line before school starts or sprinting around the playground at playtime. I'd never tell him this to his face, but one of the differences between him and Sami is that while Sami is a bit of a bulldozer, Tio is kind of graceful. When he runs, he stretches out his legs and it looks like he could almost be flying.

Then Mum mentioned my name, jolting me from my thoughts. 'I'm making pepperpot later. I'll send Ana round with some. Maybe she could walk to school with you lot. She's picking Layla up on the way, but she's not feeling quite herself today, are you, pops?'

'Sure. Morning, Ana!' Benny flashed a smile towards me. 'Kids, say hello to Ana.'

Denise was reading a book as she stood in the hallway, but her eyes flicked up briefly as she nodded at me. Sami yelled 'Hello' very loudly and Rita looked up at me with huge, brown eyes and said 'Good morning' in a serious kind of way.

Tio didn't say a word. No one noticed but me.

CASE #41029973876628

Case Holder Notes:

TUESDAY – 8.19 a.m.

Primary Subject and Primary Subject
Mother meet
Boy #1 Woman #1 Boy #2 Girl #1 Girl #2 Boy #3.
Energy Tension high.
Energy Connection very low with Boy #3.
Boy #3 = Possible Companion Subject?

TUESDAY

8.28 a.m.

I saw Layla leaning against the wall outside her dad's bike shop before she spotted us. She was wearing an incredibly large bobble hat and peering at something cupped in her hand.

She did a double take when she saw me strolling towards her with Benny's entire family. Her eyes met mine as though to ask, *What's going on?* and I tried to answer her with my eyes too: *We'll talk about it later.*

'Morning, Layla,' Benny said cheerfully.

'Morning,' Layla replied.

'What have you got there?' Benny asked.

'It's a tiny snail – a baby one,' Layla said opening her fist so we could see the snail sitting on her palm. It looked more like a little stone than anything else.

'Can I see? Can I see?' Rita said, clambering forward.

Layla kneeled down to Rita's height and we watched as a miniature feeler emerged very slowly from the snail's thin brown shell, followed by the rest of its body. It reached out towards Rita.

But then Tio loudly shouted, 'Boo!' and the snail instantly withdrew into its shell. At the same time, Sami struggled out of Benny's grip and started running ahead.

'Oh, Sami!' Benny cried. 'Tio, catch up with him, will you?'

Tio dashed away after his brother and Benny turned to me and said, 'Sorry, Ana, I'd better run after them. We'll be up ahead if you need anything.'

She rushed off with the pram and Denise and Rita by her side.

I felt my body relax as I watched them disappear up the road.

'So, what happened?' Layla asked me when we were alone, her eyes wide.

'Nothing,' I said.

'When I saw you all walking together, I thought maybe you'd said something to your mum.'

I shook my head.

'Are you okay?' she asked, her eyes still large and searching.

'I don't want to talk about it,' I replied. I had the same feeling I'd had when I was talking to Mum earlier. A loneliness coming from not being able to speak the truth.

We quietly walked together to school and I was glad that Layla didn't ask me any more about what had happened. The pavements were sparkly with frost, and some puddles had frozen over. Layla pointed at the imprint of a leaf on the ice and my worries started to melt away. But when we got to the school gates, I suddenly stopped walking. I realized I'd come to a standstill without meaning to.

Layla was distracted by the old cat who often hangs out in the school car park. She'd gone ahead to try to lure it out from under the school minibus, clicking her tongue. It came out straight away, wrapping itself around her legs.

Then Layla noticed that I'd stopped behind her. 'Ana, are you okay?' she asked.

Worry washed over me and settled in a pit at the bottom of

my stomach. I could feel people swarming past us, staring at me as I stood still in the middle of the crowd. I managed a little nod back to Layla, but I hunched over like I was trying curl myself up into a hedgehog ball and hide away. I forced my body forward, telling myself to keep going.

We managed to get into the playground and Layla and I found a quiet corner. I tried to steady my breathing, but the ball in my stomach was getting bigger and heavier with every second.

'Ana, talk to me,' Layla spoke in a gentle voice.

All of a sudden, faces in the playground seemed to surround us. A group were playing some kind of chasing game and screaming at the top of their voices each time someone got caught. I saw Tio dart past us, calling out so loudly that the sound filled my head, and I remembered the way Layla's snail had retracted into its shell when he'd shouted at it.

I tried to speak but the words got stuck in my throat.

'Can you tell me what happened yesterday?' Layla asked.

I'd come to her in tears at the end of school, but I hadn't told her anything other than that Tio had said something to upset me.

'I . . . I don't want to talk about it,' I said firmly.

'Whatever happened, it's going to be okay,' Layla said. 'You know Tio's only nasty to you because he's jealous of you.'

'Jealous of what?' I asked. What could she possibly mean?

'My mum says that when people are unkind it's because they feel insecure.'

I get a lot of advice from Layla's mum via Layla.

'He's just jealous,' Layla continued. 'I might have to say something to him.'

'Please don't, Layla,' I muttered. 'You said you wouldn't. Promise me? I couldn't hide the slight tremor in my voice. I felt a wave of worry rise up inside me. What would happen if Layla did try to talk to Tio? *He would tease you even more*, a voice in my head told me.

'Fine, but *only* because you don't want me to. But if you ever change your mind ...'

Layla may look small and timid, but she's as fierce as a flame. I've never met anyone so sure about who they are and what the right thing to do is. Sometimes when I'm dithering about something, it feels like we're opposites.

There were other ways we were different, too. Layla is one of the smallest in the class and she has the straightest mousy brown hair. But it's our different personalities that really contrast in our friendship. I like to hide away, but Layla is super confident. It sometimes looks like she's the taller one out of the two of us, because she stands up so straight.

In fact, maybe that's why we've become such close friends since she arrived at my school. She'd come to the area after her parents had separated and moved to different flats. Layla can push me to make my mind up about things, and I make her slow down and take her time. She'd only joined towards the end of the last school year, but I can't imagine her not being around; we've grown close quickly and we're always together. It's hard to remember a time before, when we weren't close, when we didn't know each other.

'Maybe you should talk to your mum,' Layla suggested.

'I don't know. She's got a big test coming up at work, and I don't want to worry her. I was thinking that maybe I would talk to Dodo.'

Layla started nodding emphatically. 'Definitely talk to Dodo. She'll know what to do.'

'She's coming round tonight,' I said. 'It's Chewy Tuesday. I could chat to her while Mum's cooking.'

'Do it,' Layla said encouragingly. 'It's bad to bury things and not talk about them.'

'Is that another of your mum's sayings?' I asked.

'Yes,' Layla said with a sheepish smile. 'But it's true.'

I looked over at Layla and felt a swell of warmth rush through me. Despite what had been happening, having Layla by my side made everything feel a whole lot better.

CASE #41029973876628

Case Holder Notes:

TUESDAY – 8.39 a.m.

Primary Subject sits with Girl #3.
Energy Tension low.
Energy Connection high.
'Friends'.

TUESDAY

10.41 a.m.

The day had begun in its usual way. We'd filed into assembly and sat cross-legged in wonky lines as Ms Bridewell-Stringer told us all about a reading challenge that was starting next week.

Then there had been reading, maths and a spelling test. I'd done all right – not amazing but not terrible either. I went over the words I'd got wrong. That's sort of how I am at school generally. I'm not naturally brilliant at anything, but I always try my hardest and that seems to work. Although, recently, I've felt like I don't even want to try. The spelling test words kept blurring in front of me, and I couldn't get them straight in my head.

At breaktime, Layla was keen to look for more snails. She wanted to see if she could find an actual snail egg and wondered what size and shape it would be. I left her looking because when she gets an idea like that, she can't think or talk about anything else. She's obsessed with animals and always thinks of questions about them that would never even occur to me.

The group from before school were playing their shouting and catching game again, being even louder than before. I was walking across the playground to see if I could find Layla – I wanted her company even if it meant getting roped into the

18

snail-egg hunt – when one of them accidentally collided with me. I fell to the ground and Mr Davies, who works with a kid a few years below me, noticed and came over to see if I was okay.

'I'm fine,' I said, although my hands felt sore and there were shooting pains pulsing through my knee. When I looked down, I saw a spot of blood beginning to bloom through the scuffed fabric of my trousers. I lifted the trouser leg carefully and saw a bloody graze glaring back at me.

'Go up and see the office for a plaster,' Mr Davies said. 'They'll clean you up.'

So that was how I ended up hobbling towards the office at breaktime, the smell of school dinners already in the air as I traipsed through the hall. Someone had started to decorate the stage on one side of the hall ready for the concert the school runs just before October half-term. It's called the Stars Concert and it's all about celebrating each of our individual talents. A few giant silver stars that I recognized from last year were hanging from the wall and someone had strung fairy lights in wonky loops between them.

The hall was currently set up for a PE lesson, but there was no one around apart from me. I waited for a few moments in the quiet. Though I knew that I needed to get to the office, and that the bell for the end of breaktime might ring at any moment, I felt myself walking towards the stage as though my legs were working independently of the voice in my head telling me what I should be doing.

It was hard to get up the steps to the stage because the pain in my knee was getting worse, but I managed to climb to the top. Then I walked out to the centre of the stage, into the spot where Ms Bridewell-Stringer stands when she gives assemblies. I could feel my palms still stinging and when I looked down at them, I saw my cut-up skin was studded with tiny stones.

I brushed the stones away and stood there for just a minute, imagining that the hall wasn't empty, but instead full of row upon row of chairs, crammed with everybody's families. That's how it would look when we had the Stars Concert before half-term. I remembered what it was like when we sang together as a class last year; a sea of shining faces looking up at me. This year, Mum and Dodo would both be there. I imagined Dodo would give me a thumbs up when I finally found their faces in the crowd and Mum would be looking at me with her big, kind, brown eyes. But as easy as it was to imagine them, the only reason I was able to stand there in that moment was because the hall was empty.

I took a deep breath. What was I doing? Part of me knew why I'd come up here and another part was telling me to get down and hurry along to the school office. But before I could question myself too much, I started to sing.

I began quietly, but it was difficult to sing in a whisper. And so, with my eyes closed, I let myself, just for a moment, fill the hall with my voice. I could feel the song reaching out to every corner of the room. It was the one we were learning for the Stars Concert, and I didn't know all the words by heart yet, but I knew the tune well enough so I just let myself sing. It felt good to do it – like all of a sudden a swarm of bees that had been buzzing around my head had been released into the air and were finally free. I could feel myself standing taller as I sang, my back uncoiling, my shoulders widening to let my lungs fill with air and release my voice into the hall.

I knew it was an odd thing to do and, like I said, if I'd thought about it too much then I'm sure I'd never have climbed up those stage steps.

If only I hadn't.

I wasn't sure what I noticed first – the squeak of a door opening or the sharp laughter that rebounded off the walls and back to me – but when I opened my eyes, I saw I wasn't alone.

Tio was there, standing in front of the stage, bent over laughing.

My voice choked into a stunted silence. I wanted to be anywhere but on the stage. There was nowhere to hide, and seeing Tio there, knowing that he'd just heard me when I thought I was alone, took my breath away. I felt like I couldn't move.

'You *really* think you can sing, huh?' he said when he'd stopped laughing.

'I—'

My whole body flooded with embarrassment; it tingled on my skin as though it were an actual burn. How could I have been so stupid? I should never have got up on the stage; I should have never opened my mouth to sing. The pain in my knee seemed to throb more and more with every passing second, and suddenly the memory from the day before filled my mind.

THE DAY BEFORE: MONDAY

3.46 p.m.

Yesterday afternoon, I'd taken the stairs back up to the classroom in twos. Layla was waiting for me in the playground while I went back to get a book I'd forgotten.

The corridors were quiet and still now that the school had emptied out for home time. There was no sign of any of the teachers either. A few things lay discarded across the shiny but scuffed floor: a snake of a scarf, an inside-out jumper and some balled up pieces of paper that looked very much like the letters about the Stars Concert that had just been handed out.

I zipped into the classroom, retrieved my book and was just about to rush back into the corridor when I heard voices.

'Here it is,' said one.

'That's not it,' said another.

'It is, it is,' said the first one. I now recognized the voice as belonging to Tio.

The thing about me and Tio is that we're more than just next-door neighbours. Although we didn't talk any more, Tio was apparently my first friend, my best friend. When we were little we went to the same nursery. Mum told me that we used to follow each other around all the time, and if anyone else tried to play with me, Tio would start crying.

But now, overhearing him in the corridor outside, I froze and held my breath.

I couldn't pinpoint exactly when it had started, but I was pretty sure Tio didn't like me any more. It started off as a collection of small things that on their own might seem like nothing at all, but when I put them all together they made me certain that we were most definitely not friends now.

There was his birthday, a few weeks into term, when he brought in packets of sweets for everyone. It's always a bit of a rush at the end of the day and Tio was running around giving out sweets while our class teacher, Ms Randall, was handing out slips for a school trip. Tio missed me out and I was sure it was on purpose.

Then a month ago, he started laughing out loud when I was trying (and failing) to answer a question in class. My voice dried up completely and I could feel tears suddenly ready to spring from my eyes. Ms Randall was furious and told him she wanted to talk to him during breaktime. He'd huffed and said it was about something else, nothing at all to do with me, but I knew that was lie.

I had a long list of things like this, little things really, but whenever I put them together it made me sure Tio no longer liked me.

Tio even made a comment today when Ms Randall had told us about the concert. She'd asked if anyone thought they wanted to sing a solo or in a small group, and I'd raised my hand. But then Tio glanced round and noticed my hand up, so I put it down straight away.

'Ana wants to do it,' he said in a loud, flat tone.

Ms Randall looked over at me.

'Do you, Ana? That would be really great.'

I shook my head. 'No, I didn't put my hand up, I was just ...'

'You did!' Tio said.

'I didn't.'

'You did!' he insisted.

'Tio!' Ms Randall said in a steely voice. 'Whatever you saw, I'm asking Ana now and that's final.' She looked over at me and said, 'In fact, you don't need to tell me now, Ana. Have a think about it. And that goes for everyone else, too.'

'I know I saw you,' Tio whispered under his breath.

I stayed facing forward and focused on a tiny patch of Ms Randall's yellow jumper. The truth was, when Ms Randall had mentioned that there might be the opportunity for a few of us to sing a little bit of the song at the concert either as a solo or a small group, I'd felt something light up inside me. All I knew then was that I wanted to give it a try.

But as soon as Tio noticed me volunteering, the other voice came rolling through my mind: *You'll embarrass yourself, you won't be good enough, don't even try and then people won't know you can't do it.*

I'd managed to avoid seeing Tio for the rest of the day, but now I was stuck in the classroom unable to leave because I knew he was outside. I heard some scuffling out in the corridor and wondered, hoped, that Tio and whoever he was with were leaving. I took a little step towards the door.

'Did you see Ana put her hand up for the solo today?' Tio

said all of a sudden. I shrank down where I was standing. It was like he was able to read my mind. *But he doesn't even know I'm in here*, I told myself, although I ducked behind a chair just in case.

'She can't sing any better than that mangy old cat that always hangs around the car park,' Tio declared.

The other person didn't reply.

'Oh, I'm Ana. I think I'm the best. I think I can do anything,' blared Tio. He wouldn't let it rest.

The other person put on a silly voice and joined in: 'I'm Ana, I think I can sing better than anyone.' I realized it was Chidi.

'I'm Ana. I'll do the solo.'

'I'm Ana. I want everyone to look at me.'

'I'm Ana. I have to be the centre of attention.'

'I'm Ana, I'm Ana, I'm Ana.'

They kept going on and on and on in an awful chant. I wanted to leave but there was no way out except past them. I wanted to hide but there was nowhere to conceal me. And I wanted to look, too. I wanted to see the awfulness of the words spilling from their mouths. It was like poking a bruise.

I took a few little steps back towards the classroom door and peeked as far round as I dared to catch a glimpse of Tio and Chidi stomping back and forth down the corridor, their voices ringing out. Tio had picked up the scarf from the floor and wrapped one end around his neck, the rest trailing behind him. Sometimes he'd stop to fling it out so it would fly into the air for just a second as though it were a tail lashing out.

Then I heard another voice: Ms Randall's.

'What are you two still doing up here?'

'Nothing, miss,' said Chidi.

'Just getting my jumper, miss,' said Tio.

I waited until everyone's footsteps had disappeared before I stood up and trailed down the stairs to Layla, a feeling of dread weighing me down with every step.

TUESDAY

10.53 a.m.

Now here I was, standing on the stage, Tio directly in front of me. There was no escape, just like when I'd been stuck in the classroom yesterday. He was holding his sides as though they ached from laughing.

'That was absolutely the worst thing that I've ever heard in my whole life.' Every word he spoke seemed to strike me physically, each one a separate blow.

'I ... I ...' I was suddenly incapable of speaking, although there were dozens of replies racing through my mind: *I didn't think anyone would hear me, I especially didn't want you to hear, I know I'm no good at singing, I wish I'd never put my hand up yesterday, I wish I'd never got on this stage to see whether I might be able to do it because I can't, I won't ever, I'll never do it.*

'Surely you don't think you can really sing at the concert? In front of everyone?'

I still stood there, voiceless.

At that moment one of the newer teachers, Mr Burton, pushed through the door, staggering under the bulk of a huge bag of colourful footballs. He was already well known in the school for being terrible at telling people off.

'Umm, you shouldn't be up there,' he stammered when he saw me on the stage.

'Her name's Ana,' Tio said. 'She's in 6R.'

'I don't think you should be in here either,' Mr Burton said uncertainly to Tio.

'But, Mr B!' Tio said. 'I was just walking through with a note for Ms Scanlan when I saw Ana on the stage – *illegally*. I was telling *her* that she should get down.'

'It's not illegal.' Mr Burton was flustered, starting to struggle to keep hold of the large bag of balls. 'It's just not allowed.'

'You should tell Ms Randall about it, though. That's her teacher, sir,' Tio continued. 'I don't know how long she'd been up there, *illegally*.'

I felt his words like I'd been stung.

'I'm ... I might speak to Ms Randall later, I'm just ... I'm going to drop these ...' And as he said it, he shifted his arm ever so slightly so that the bag lurched to one side and balls started spilling out across the hall in every direction.

Mr Burton gave a shout of exasperation, and as he did, more balls fell to the floor and bounced away.

'Ana will help you,' Tio suggested. 'To say sorry for being on the stage when she wasn't meant to be.'

Mr Burton didn't seem to hear Tio as he struggled to hold on to the few balls left in the bag, but then I saw him glance towards me.

'Come on, Ana,' I heard Tio say. 'You'd better help out or you'll get into big trouble.'

I walked down the stairs of the stage and kneeled to pick up a ball that had rolled to a stop near me. Just then, Tio kicked a ball in my direction with full force, but it skimmed past me before it hit the wall with a thump. Then he walked away, still making the sound of a laugh that wasn't really a laugh at all.

I watched him as he stalked out of the hall. Tio was so familiar to me from all our years growing up together, but in that moment he was like a stranger.

I couldn't help but think of the questions that had been haunting me ever since Tio had changed towards me: *How can we have grown so far apart? And what have I done to cause it?*

CASE #41029973876628

Case Holder Notes:

TUESDAY – 10.55 a.m.

Primary Subject Energy Tension extremely high.
   Companion Subject confirmed: Boy #3.
   Proceed to checks.

TUESDAY

12.32 p.m.

'What happened?' Layla asked as we sat across the table from each other at lunch.

I was being careful not to knock my knee against the table or Layla's legs because it was still sore and bloody. After seeing Tio in the hall, I'd hurried back to class even though breaktime wasn't over and I hadn't been to the office to show anyone my injuries. I didn't think I would be able to speak without crying. In our next lesson, I could feel Layla's eyes on me, and I'd whispered to her when Ms Randall was fiddling with the whiteboard that I'd fallen over in the playground.

'It's nothing,' I said. I had the empty feeling that was getting very familiar now.

'It's not nothing, Ana. You've not been right since yesterday and then something happened over breaktime – more than you just hurting your knee – I know it.' A mixture of frustration and worry spread across Layla's face.

'It was … it was … so stupid …' I began.

'Tell me,' she said softly.

I hesitated, but I did want Layla to know what had happened.

'You know yesterday when Tio said he saw me put up my hand for the concert?'

'And you said that you didn't,' Layla added.

'Well, I was lying. I did raise my hand. I thought for a second that maybe I could do it: sing on my own or with a couple of other people at the concert.'

Layla opened her mouth to speak, and I knew that she was going to tell me that she believed I could too, but I hurried on with my story.

'But as soon as Tio spotted me, I knew it was a stupid idea. And then when I went back to get my book after school, I over-heard him talking about how terrible I was at singing. And I don't know why, but as I was walking through the hall at breaktime today, I thought that if I went on stage for just a minute, it might help me decide if I did want to sing at the concert or whether it was definitely a bad idea.'

Layla nodded, and I continued, glad she hadn't interrupted me. 'So I did it. There was no one around and I stood in the middle of the stage and sang a few words.'

Layla nodded again. I loved her for not saying that was a terrible idea.

'But Tio was there. He came in and heard me, and he wouldn't stop laughing.'

Layla's hazel eyes flashed dark. Her expression changed from attentive to fierce. 'I've had enough of this,' she said, standing up and scanning the lunch hall.

'Layla, please don't,' I said in a panic.

'But it's not okay, Ana. He's bullying you and it can't carry on. Like I said before, this is all to do with him, and nothing to do with you.'

She looked over at the back table where Tio was sitting and marched towards him.

I tried to catch up with her, but she dashed in between the tables and was standing in front of Tio before I could reach her.

'Apologize to Ana,' I heard Layla say as I approached behind her.

Tio gave a sideways smile to Chidi who was sitting next to him. 'What makes you think I'm going to do that?'

'You've upset her,' Layla said, standing her ground. 'So you need to say sorry.'

Tio looked up at Layla with narrowed eyes. 'I haven't done anything to upset her.'

'You laughed at her when she was sing—'

'Look, anyone would have. You weren't there. You didn't hear how bad she sounded,' Tio interrupted, looking smug.

I could see Layla's fists clench into tight balls, but I felt myself shrinking behind her, hunching over once again as though I could hide from everyone in the room.

'She was only singing on the stage because she was trying to see if she wanted to perform at the concert. She's got more guts than you'll ever know,' Layla carried on, her voice firm.

'It'd be better if she only sang in private,' Tio said quickly with a smirk.

'You're ... you're horrible, Tio,' Layla blurted. 'You think you're so great and funny and that everyone loves you, but it's all in your head.'

For a split second Tio's eyes flashed with hurt, but the next moment it vanished and his expression changed to one of swelling confidence. 'It's all in Ana's head, you mean. I know you're her friend and everything, but honestly, have you ever even heard her sing?'

33

Layla faltered for just a moment and Tio clapped his hands together with glee. 'You haven't, have you? You haven't heard her sing! Honestly, you don't know how bad it is. I'm doing her a favour by telling her. I'm being a better friend to her than you are.'

Everyone's eyes were on me, and though the hall was noisy with the lunchtime din, it seemed to grow quiet in those few seconds. I felt a jolt of white-hot shame run through me and all I could hear was the beating of my own heart.

'You don't know what you're talking about,' Layla retorted, but it was too late. The damage had been done. Everyone knew that, for once, Layla didn't know what she was talking about.

TUESDAY

3.32 p.m.

'Ana, wait up,' Layla called after me as I rushed out of the class-room at the end of the day.

I'd been willing the clock hands to move faster all afternoon, but those few hours had dragged on for so long that I wondered if school would ever finish. I knew that Ms Randall had sensed there was something wrong. She'd even asked me in a quiet voice if I was feeling okay. Someone overheard on the table next to me and they whispered to the person sitting next to them. They'd tittered together, looking over at me. What had happened between me and Tio had spread through the whole class by the end of lunchtime. I overheard Susie talking about it when we lined up to come back in for the afternoon, and I could feel every-one staring at me. It made me feel angry with Layla, somehow. If she hadn't gone over and caused a big fuss, then things wouldn't have been so bad. Now everyone knew what I'd done.

'I just want to get home,' I said to Layla through clenched teeth.

'Ana, I'm sorry ... I thought that ... it would help.'

I couldn't meet Layla's gaze. Though I knew she was on my side, what she'd said had made everyone think I really was the worst singer in the world.

I was never going to sing again. It was that simple. I'd decided it that afternoon, and though it felt like a prickly decision to hold on to, I couldn't see any other way forward.

'I know,' I said flatly. 'But I asked you not to, and you did it anyway. Now everyone knows about what happened.'

Layla's face went blank and she paled. 'I'm sorry,' she said in a whisper.

'I want to be alone,' I said firmly. I turned away from her then and walked as quickly as I could on my injured knee.

CASE #41029973876628

Case Holder Notes:

TUESDAY – 5.53 p.m.

Primary Subject Energy Tension dropping
but still high.
Primary Subject sits alone.

TUESDAY

6.06 p.m.

'That'll be Dodo,' Mum said when we heard a knock on the front door.

I'd spent the last couple of hours unsuccessfully doing my homework and trying to ignore the gnawing worry about going back to school the next day and facing everyone. I wouldn't be able to pretend that I wasn't well again. But I knew seeing Dodo would make me feel a little more cheerful, and maybe I'd be able to speak to her about what had been happening. Maybe she'd be able to help.

I scrambled up to greet her, but as Mum swung the door open, I heard her speak in a tone that told me straight away that it wasn't Dodo.

She shut the door and turned towards me looking slightly quizzical. 'Just someone about a charity,' she said and then looked at her watch.

'Do you think Dodo's okay?' I asked, reading Mum's face.

'Sure she is. She's probably just stuck in traffic. Here, take this over to Benny and her lot while we wait, would you?'

Mum ladled some stew from the huge saucepan into one of the dishes with a lid that usually sits at the back of the cupboard. Mum has been doing this for Benny every now and then since Mario was born, because she says Benny has enough going on, and that it's a small thing we can do to help. She always asks me to take it round, even though I'm never able to hide how much I don't want to.

'I can't,' I said, looking for something to do. I lunged for my school bag and started to dig around inside it for a book. 'I've got loads more homework to finish.'

'Well, it'll only take you a second and then you can keep going,' Mum said.

'I-I—'

Mum turned round so she was facing me, a kind but questioning look on her face. 'Is something up?' she asked. 'You can talk to me about it if there is ...'

I looked up at her, and in that moment, Mum's face seemed so full of sadness that I thought she might start to cry. She seemed to know that I'd spotted her expression, because she suddenly looked away from me. But not before I noticed the lines of tiredness around her eyes. They'd become worse since she'd started getting up earlier than usual to revise.

'No, nothing's up,' I said. I tried to smile and sound normal, but there was a tightness in my voice I couldn't hide. 'I'll take the stew over.'

'Are you sure? It's quite heavy, actually,' Mum said. 'Maybe I should do it.'

'No, I can manage,' I replied, although it was quite difficult to lift, even with two hands.

Mum opened the door for me and I could feel her watching as I walked down the corridor, but when I looked back, she shrank into the doorway. I had no free hand to knock on Benny's door, so I had to use my foot to tap at it.

I could hear a flurry of voices from inside the flat, and I tried to arrange my face to look neutral. It could be Benny, I thought. Or Denise. Or even Sami or Rita. It didn't have to be Tio.

But the door swung open to reveal Tio looking grumpily at me. I thought his eyes flashed with surprise for just a moment when he saw it was me, but then his expression changed to one of boredom and disinterest.

'My mum sent me over with this,' I said and held out the stew towards him.

Tio hesitated, like he didn't even want to take the dish, but then I heard Benny's voice in the background and he reached for it.

'What is it?' he said.

'Pepperpot,' I answered.

I turned to go, but then Benny was at the door. 'Thank you, Ana,' she said kindly. 'Be sure to say a big thank you to your mum, too.'

I nodded.

'Tio,' Benny prodded. 'What do you say?'

'Thanks,' Tio said quickly, through gritted teeth.

'Do you want to come in, Ana?' Benny said. 'Tio's playing that game you're all into at the moment.'

'No, I'm not,' Tio said at the same time as I said, 'I've got to get back for dinner.'

Just then, the baby started to cry and Rita shouted out, 'Mumma, Mumma,' over and over, like she was a car alarm.

'Well, another time, then,' Benny said. She looked from Tio to me and then back to Tio. 'I'll leave you two to say goodbye, but do thank your mum. And you should come round again soon, and stay next time.'

'Maybe I will,' I agreed over the bawling of Mario and Rita, although I didn't mean it.

Benny stepped away, leaving me and Tio alone.

'Bye—' I started to say but the front door slammed shut.

I could hear Tio's voice quietly but clearly through the door: 'Hopefully never.'

I stared at the closed door for a moment, unmoving. How can two words make you feel like you've been punched in the gut? Whatever hope I still held that Tio and I could ever make up disappeared.

TUESDAY

6.36 p.m.

When Dodo still hadn't turned up, Mum handed me her phone and said, 'Why don't you give her a call and see where she is?'

I'd been pretending to do my homework since I'd delivered the stew next door, but I hadn't been able to concentrate. I'd felt like I had a storm inside me since Tio had slammed the door shut in my face.

I pressed the button to connect the call and waited for Dodo to answer. It rang for so long that I was sure it was about to go to voicemail, but then someone picked up.

'Hello?'

'Dodo?' I asked.

'Ana?'

'Yes,' I said. There was a pause of a moment or two when neither of us said a word. Then we both started speaking at the same time. I said, 'We were calling to see if you were on your way over,' and Dodo said something about just waking up.

'Are you okay?' I asked in a worried voice.

'I think I have a bit of a bug, but I'm fine. It's nice to hear from you, my Ana Ban-ana.'

Dodo hadn't called me that since I asked her a few years ago to stop because it had started to feel a bit silly, but just then it was nice to hear her old nickname for me.

'It's Tuesday, so . . .' I said.

'Goodness, Tuesday already. It feels like Monday didn't even happen.'

'It's Chewy Tuesday,' I reiterated.

'Chewy Tuesday? Goodness, what's that?' Dodo said.

I laughed nervously. Mum looked over and met my eye. 'Is she okay?' she mouthed. I made a face and mouthed back: 'I don't know.'

'Chewy Tuesday,' I prompted Dodo again. 'When we eat together. It's our turn to cook this week. Mum's made pepperpot.'

'Mmm, pepperpot,' Dodo said back.

'So . . . are you coming over?' I asked.

'I suppose I could,' Dodo said. 'I do like pepperpot.'

'Well, see you soon, then,' I said.

'Okay, Ana Ban-ana,' Dodo replied and hung up.

'What happened?' Mum asked. She was halfway through drying up. The kitchen was spotless despite the frenzy of cooking that Mum had done that afternoon.

'She's coming over now,' I replied, but I said it in a way that made it sound like a question.

'Are you sure she's all right?' Mum asked.

'I think so . . . but she did she seem a little bit funny,' I said.

'Funny how?' Mum put down the glass and the tea towel and looked over at me.

'She didn't seem to know what Chewy Tuesday was,' I said. 'But she must have just been kidding.'

Mum pursed her lips. 'Hmm. Did she say she was on her way?'

'I think she said she was about to leave,' I muttered, although I didn't sound certain.

I had the weirdest feeling that Dodo hadn't been able to understand me properly. It felt like we weren't hearing each other, or sentences were being missed out somehow. It was the strangest conversation I'd ever had with her.

Mum checked her watch again. 'Okay, so she'll be here for just after seven.'

'Yes,' I said. But I couldn't shake the feeling that something wasn't right.

TUESDAY

7.47 p.m.

The food had already been ladled into serving bowls and placed in the middle of the table. Mum had even packed away her books. The pepperpot had been steaming when Mum first put it out, but now it was cold and looked jellified.

'Where is she?' Mum asked and checked her phone again. We'd rung Dodo a few times, but it kept going through to voicemail. Mum drummed her fingers against the table, then started scrolling.

'What are you doing?'

'I'm going to call Jenna,' Mum said. 'To check on Dodo.'

Jenna was one of Dodo's neighbours. Mum had been in contact with her before over something to do with a job at the hospital. I heard Mum get through to Jenna and tell her we were worried about Dodo. She explained that we couldn't get through to her and that she'd forgotten all about our weekly dinner. Mum asked if she could go over to see if Dodo was there, and talked Jenna through where to find the spare key for the door (hidden under one of the flowerpots). A few moments later, Mum's face drained of colour.

'Is she waking up? Is she waking up?' Mum's voice rose higher and higher.

There was a long pause and then Mum said, 'Okay. I'm coming over right away. Can you call an ambulance and wait with her, please? I should be there by the time they arrive, but if I'm not, make sure you mention the memory loss to them.' They spoke for a few more moments before she hung up.

'What's happening, Mum?' I asked, but my voice came out shaky. Something was wrong with Dodo – I'd been right to worry earlier. My mind started racing through all the things that could have happened. I felt as though the ground was suddenly shifting beneath me, tilting the room as if the walls were sliding around.

'Hopefully nothing, but it's best to be on the safe side. It seems like Dodo had gone to bed.'

'Bed?' I squeaked. She was meant to be on her way over, so I couldn't understand why she'd have done that.

'Yes. Apparently she was in her pyjamas and everything.'

'But, but . . .' I stuttered.

'I know. I'm going to check on her.'

'I'm coming with you,' I insisted.

'Ana, I don't think that's a good idea. I don't know how long I'll be or . . .' She didn't finish the sentence. 'Why don't you go and stay with Benny and her kids for the rest of the evening. I don't want to leave you here alone.'

'No. No way,' I said, anger starting to bubble inside me. 'I'm coming with you. You can't make me stay here with them.'

Mum looked at me and then glanced at her phone. I saw her hesitate for a moment, and it was just long enough for me to jump in again and say, 'I'm coming with you. Even if you leave me behind, I'll follow you. I want to check on Dodo, too.'

'All right,' Mum said. 'But if I need to go to the hospital with

46

her, then you might need to stay overnight somewhere else. Maybe I can call Tully. Layla's with her tonight, right?'

A sinking feeling overcame me as I remembered how I'd left things with Layla. It felt like I was lugging a heavy grey stone around with me. We'd never fallen out before, and I couldn't shift Layla's hurt expression from my mind. What with everything that was happening with Tio, falling out with Layla and then whatever was wrong with Dodo, today had turned into the worst day ever.

'Yeah, I can stay with Layla if I need to,' I lied.

I felt a trickle of apprehension, but this time I wasn't sure who it was for: Tio, Layla, or now Dodo.

TUESDAY

9.04 p.m.

'I'm fine, Letts. Honestly I am,' Dodo said. She sipped at the cup of hot milk Mum had made for her then pulled a face.

'Drink it all up, little sister,' Mum said sternly. Mum's a couple of years older than Dodo and sometimes she likes to remind her of that fact.

Dodo made a face at Mum but took another sip.

'And eat that last piece,' Mum said, pushing the plate of crumbs and the last triangle of toast towards her.

The ambulance had already arrived by the time Mum and I got to Dodo's and we'd run all the way up to her flat. She'd been sitting on her sofa wearing her oversized pyjamas and hairy blue cardigan, looking into a light that the paramedic was shining into her eyes. Mum and Jenna had a whispered conversation in the corner and I stayed quiet, straining to listen. Jenna told Mum that it had taken a little while for Dodo's memory to come back, and it had been scary when she'd woken her up and Dodo didn't know who or where she was.

My ears pricked up at that. Dodo hadn't known who she was? No wonder Mum had hurried over here and they'd called an ambulance. My eyes moved to Dodo, who was still on the sofa.

She was nodding at the questions the paramedic was asking her, but she must have felt me looking at her because she met my eye. She smiled and pulled a funny face, the way she always did to get a grin out of me. Dodo then gave a little nod towards the woman that seemed to tell me, 'I want to talk to you, but I've got to do this for a tiny bit longer, then I'll be with you.'

Soon after that, the paramedics left, saying that everything was fine, but they couldn't explain the blanks in Dodo's memory. Mum said they'd contact the GP the next day to get a referral, but everyone agreed that for now she was okay. Then Jenna left too, saying we could call at any time if Dodo needed anything.

Once we were alone, Dodo had opened her arms to me. 'Come here, Ana Ban-ana.'

I sank into her hairy blue cardigan that smelled like pancakes and flowers. I could hear Mum in the kitchen, along with the beep of the microwave and the noise of toast popping up. She'd insisted that Dodo have a cup of hot milk and that we all have something to eat.

'I was worried about you. Are you all right?' I said very quietly into the blue fluff.

At first I thought she hadn't heard me, but then she kissed the very top of my head and said, 'You don't have to worry about me.'

Then Mum had come in with the milk and toast and made Dodo drink and eat.

As soon as she'd swallowed her last mouthful of toast, Mum had started with her questions.

'What's the last thing you can remember?'

'Umm . . . I think it's setting up the camera trap on the Polden Road estate,' Dodo said.

'From yesterday night?' Mum asked sharply.

I knew that Dodo often set up camera traps in the city for her job as a naturalist so she could study which animals were visiting certain areas.

'Yes. I can remember putting the camera in place. It's completely deserted there because they're knocking the estate down. I remember thinking how peaceful it was. I think that's the last clear thing I've got. Since then, I've been feeling really foggy.'

'Why didn't you call me?' Mum said.

'I didn't realize how bad it was,' Dodo said. 'And anyway, I was okay. I got myself home, didn't I? There are just a few things that I can't remember, that's all. But I don't think I quite realized I couldn't remember them.'

Mum didn't answer, although I could see from her face that there was a lot that she wanted to say.

'What about when we spoke on the phone tonight?' I jumped in. Even though Dodo seemed okay, and I felt better for seeing her, I couldn't shift the worry that sat in my stomach. 'When I told you about the pepperpot and you said you were coming round.'

Dodo looked worried and she shook her head.

'And Chewy Tuesdays?' I said.

'No, I do remember them now,' Dodo said. 'Last week we ate here, right?'

'That's right,' Mum said. She gave Dodo an appraising look. 'How have you been sleeping recently?'

'Oh, you know,' Dodo said vaguely.

'No, I don't know,' Mum said tightly. 'That's why I'm asking.'

'It's not been great recently,' Dodo mumbled.

'Well, maybe that has something to do with it,' Mum suggested. I knew Dodo suffered from insomnia, which meant she found it difficult to go to sleep sometimes. This week must have been particularly bad to make her behave so strangely.

'Do you think you've been working too much recently?' Mum continued to question her.

'Too much?' Dodo replied.

'You know how you get,' Mum said, looking away from Dodo.

A slightly uneasy silence followed. I could see Dodo sit up as though she wanted to say something, but she kept quiet. Her face flushed with an expression I couldn't quite pinpoint: anger, upset, hurt or sadness.

I don't like it when they speak like this; there always seems to be a lot they aren't saying to each other. It frustrates me, but I know how sometimes it's easier not to talk about what's really on your mind.

Finally, Dodo broke the silence: 'Hey, Ana. Do you want to see pictures of the fox family I found, while you're here?'

I nodded. Dodo had told us last week that she'd found a den with five foxes – two vixens and three cubs – somewhere near the railway embankment.

'I'm just going to the toilet and then we'd better head off. It's a school night after all,' Mum said.

'Here.' Dodo motioned to me, ignoring Mum and opening up one of her notebooks. She pulled out a pile of printouts and spaced them out carefully into a grid on the table. 'That's the mother,' Dodo said, pointing to a thin fox with glowing eyes. 'She's a real strong one. And this is the other vixen. They share the responsibility of looking after the cubs and finding food. This other vixen is probably her daughter, or maybe a sister. And here are the cubs – playing together.' She looked at them fondly and traced a finger over one of their tails.

Her notebook lay open at an angle and I could see some of Dodo's drawings of the foxes in there too.

'Hey, those are really good,' I said, attracted more to Dodo's sketches than to the photos. They made the foxes look like they were about to spring off the page somehow.

'Thanks,' Dodo said. She looked over my shoulder as I flicked through the book. 'They're a bit rough.'

Dodo had written an unfamiliar word next to each of her fox drawings. 'What does that mean?' I asked, pointing to it. '*Vulps ... vulps.*' I stumbled over the pronunciation.

'It's *Vulp-es vulp-es. Vulpes vulpes* is the Latin name for foxes,' Dodo explained. 'There are a few animals where the name repeats itself for the creature – *Gorilla gorilla* ... you can guess what that is. Or *Lutra lutra* – that's an otter. *Pica pica* is a magpie.'

Dodo listed other animals that had that type of Latin name, and I could tell she was starting to feel better. Her voice was calmer, and she sounded much more like herself.

I glanced towards the corridor where I could see the bathroom door was still closed. Mum could come back any minute, but I wondered if I could use this moment to tell Dodo about what had been happening with Tio at school. I felt certain she'd be able to help me, or maybe, like Layla had said, just talking about it would help.

But then I turned another page of the notebook and saw a different type of creature entirely. Dodo had drawn it using hard, black scribbles. She'd pressed down on the paper so much that it was dented from the pressure. It was unlike any other creature I'd seen before – it looked more like a shadow than anything else, but it had long tentacle arms that protruded from its body, and they swirled out wide, filling the page.

'What's that?' I asked suspiciously. Something about the creature made me feel odd.

Dodo frowned a little. 'I don't know exactly. I think it came into my head and I had to draw it. I can't really remember doing it. It shouldn't be in there anyway.'

She reached for the page and tore it out neatly, but as she did, I saw that underneath it, on the next page, there was another black scribbled drawing of the creature. I turned to the page after that. There was another drawing. And another. I flicked through to the end of the notebook – it was filled with them.

'Goodness, I really don't remember drawing all those. It must have come from one of my funny dreams,' Dodo said uncertainly. She held the drawing that she'd torn out of the book, and for just a second I saw her hands tremble. But the next moment, she'd scrunched it up into a ball and buried it deep in the pocket of her cardigan, just as Mum walked back in.

'Are you all done here?' Mum asked. 'We'd better get going.'

Dodo closed the notebook quickly. 'Yes, all done,' she said.

'Try to get some rest, Dodo,' Mum said. 'Promise me?'

'Yes, Letts,' Dodo said before reaching out to hug Mum. Then Dodo turned to me. 'Thanks, Ana Ban-ana,' she said and wrapped me in a hug too. 'Hold on, you don't like it when I call you that any more, do you?'

'It's okay,' I said. 'I think I like it again.'

She tried to smile to reassure me that everything was fine, but her face looked pinched, almost as if she was trying to process something that she herself couldn't quite understand.

As we left, I couldn't shake the feeling that despite Dodo seeming better, there was still something very wrong.

TUESDAY

11.27 p.m.

A bleeping tune woke me. I was dreaming I was in a circus that was also a zoo, and the tune seemed to be coming from the carousel ride. But in my dream, the carousel horses were actually real elephants and lions, and they were roaring and bellowing and trying to escape. As I blinked myself awake, I realized I was in my bedroom and that the music was, in fact, coming from the living room.

I stumbled from bed out into the hall and towards the sound, and found Mum's phone lit up, charging in one of the sockets. I reached for it and saw Dodo was calling.

As I answered the videocall, the screen filled with an image of Dodo's face. She was no longer in her pyjamas and her hairy blue cardigan, nor was she in the soft light of her cosy living room. The light was white and harsh and there was a large plant with spiky leaves behind her that I'd never seen before at her flat.

'Ana,' she said, 'go get your mum.' She looked scared, so scared that I didn't ask any questions. I pulled the charging cord from the phone and ran into Mum's bedroom, almost tripping over her clothes on the floor.

'Mum. Mum! It's Dodo.'

Mum didn't stir. She looked deeply asleep.

'Mum,' I said again and prodded her.

She still didn't move, and I had the overwhelming urge to shake her with even more force. I was panicking that she might not wake up, but in the next moment she sat bolt upright and seemed to be fully awake.

'Ana! What's wrong?' she asked. 'Are you okay?'

'It's Dodo,' I repeated and held out the phone to her. Mum plucked it from my hand and asked Dodo the very same questions: *What's wrong? Are you okay?*

'I can't . . .' Dodo began to say. She looked over her shoulder. 'I'm not sure it's safe to talk. I'm okay, I'm okay. I'll call you in the morning.' Then she hung up.

Mum looked at the blank screen of her phone, worry filling her face. I had the same prickling feeling of anxiety I'd had earlier that night. I'd known something wasn't right with Dodo when we'd left her. Now she said it wasn't safe to talk. Didn't that mean that she was in some sort of danger?

'What's happened?' I asked.

But Mum, usually so sure and certain, looked lost and pale. 'I don't know, pops. I don't know.'

Her fingers fumbled the phone as she rang Dodo back.

But Dodo didn't pick up.

TUESDAY

11.44 p.m.

'She'll be fine,' Mum said. I'd lost track of how many times she'd said that now. She passed me a cup of hot milk, just like the one she'd given to Dodo a few hours earlier.

'But she didn't look fine,' I said. 'She looked . . . scared.'

Mum took a deep breath. 'You're right, she did.'

'And where was she? She wasn't at home.'

'I think she was in her office,' Mum said. 'Who knows why she's gone there at this time of night. She must have been struggling with insomnia again.'

'And you think that's why she lost some of her memory – because she hasn't been sleeping well?' I asked.

'I don't know, really, but it can't help. It's never good to not get enough sleep or rest. Our bodies and minds need it so much.'

'I don't think I'm going to be able to fall asleep now,' I replied, a wobble creeping into my voice.

'Yes, you are,' Mum said, soothingly. 'You're going to drink the rest of that cup of milk and we'll get you nice and comfy. You'll fall asleep before you know it.'

'But I'm worried about Dodo,' I said.

'I know.' Mum looked me right in the eye. 'Listen, this is what

I'm going to do. I'm going to call the local police and ask if they'll check Dodo's office because she's not been herself this evening. I'll ask them to bring her over here so we can look after her. I'd go myself, but I can't leave you alone and I don't want to wake up anyone else right now. It'll be okay. You don't need to worry about it, pops.'

'Will the police really go to look for her?'

'Yes,' Mum said. 'I'll explain what happened this evening and why we're concerned. When you wake up in the morning, Dodo will probably be here snoring on the sofa, and we'll feel silly for being so worried.'

Mum tucked me up after I'd drunk the milk, and she was right, I did feel warm and safe all bunched up in my duvet in bed. It was like being in a bird's nest.

She kissed me on the forehead and said, 'Sleep tight, pops.'

A few moments later, I heard Mum speaking on the phone.

She's ringing the police, I thought. I strained my ears to listen, but she was speaking too softly. Then she went quiet but the light in the living room stayed on. *She must be waiting up for the police to bring Dodo over.*

I tried to burrow down into my bed to make myself comfortable. I thought I'd need to wait until I heard Dodo arrive before I'd be able fall asleep. But whether it was the hot milk, being tucked up in bed or everything that had happened that evening, I found myself fighting to stay awake. I felt so exhausted – it was a huge effort to keep my eyes open. I tried to keep myself awake until I heard Dodo's voice, but it wasn't long until I drifted off.

CASE #41029973876628

Case Holder Notes:

WEDNESDAY – 7.43 a.m.

Initiate wake-up.

WEDNESDAY

7.43 a.m.

I woke with a gasp and lurched forward in bed. I'd come to mid-dream, and I felt like I could *almost* remember it as my eyes flickered open. It was something to do with winter: darkness filling the sky and a feeling of cold going on and on. But as soon as I tried to think about it properly, it slipped away from me and became so distant and vague that it was suddenly unimaginable.

I rubbed my eyes a little and looked around my room. Something was different. Maybe an object had been moved, but after a few minutes of checking carefully, I couldn't work out what had changed so I gave up trying.

It was my same old room, with piles of clothes on the floor and overdue library books stacked up in the corner. I could still make out the stains on the carpet from when Dodo brought round a dog she was looking after. It had tracked mud all through the flat. We'd scrubbed and scrubbed, but we couldn't quite shift it.

Dodo. Last night's events flooded back to me and I swung my legs from the bed, pulling the curtains open in two quick swipes, only glancing outside for a second.

I didn't see it then. I didn't notice anything odd.

But the world had stopped.

WEDNESDAY

7.49 a.m.

I rushed into the living room but it was completely still. Mum wasn't up yet. And there was no lump on the sofa buried under blankets – Dodo wasn't here either. I peered into Mum's bedroom but she was unmoving. I could tell she was in a deep sleep from the sound of her breathing. I wondered if she'd been up late talking to the police and to Dodo and that's why she wasn't awake. She'd usually be at the table by now, focused on revising. Dodo must be back at her flat, I told myself, or Mum would already be awake.

So I did all the normal morning tasks – I got dressed, went to the bathroom, then looked around for something for breakfast. My stomach was growling, and I remembered that I hadn't eaten much last night. We'd only had toast for dinner at Dodo's. It was, Dodo said, the world's worst Chewy Tuesday, until we reminded her of the brownies and how Mum had needed to visit the dentist afterwards.

I tipped cereal into a bowl, but it was the end of the box so there were only the dusty bits left at the bottom of the bag. I mixed them up with milk, then ate that along with a banana from the fruit bowl.

It was quiet in the flat, unusually so without Mum up and about. I could only hear the sounds I was making as I shuffled around. I didn't want to wake Mum, so I didn't turn on the television.

I got everything ready to leave for school and was almost out of the door when I had an alarming thought – I hadn't heard next door's baby yet. At this time in the morning we could usually hear Mario's squawks or crying through the walls.

But today he was quiet. I didn't even hear any voices talking – sometimes I overheard Sami shouting or Denise yelling or even Tio's voice.

In any case, even by the time I left our flat and rode the lift all the way down to the ground floor, it hadn't struck me as odd that no one else was around. Because I was alone in the lift, I started humming softly to myself without realizing. It was the song that we'd been learning for the Stars Concert, and the memory of standing on the stage in front of Tio rushed back to me. But as the lift continued to travel down, I felt safe – hidden and insulated – in the little metal box. Surely no one would be able to hear me and I'd know to fall silent if the lift slowed to stop at a floor. I grew louder and louder with each breath, filling my lungs to reach for the right notes. I sang so loudly that, just for a moment, it felt like the lift might begin shaking from the sound of my voice. I felt a lightness rush through me and my shoulders rose up from their usual slumped position. I let myself stand tall.

In that moment, it felt so good to block out all my worries and just let myself sing. I started to think that all the things I'd been worrying about would work themselves out. We'd take care of Dodo, I could make up with Layla and find out what was wrong between Tio and me ... but then my thoughts skidded to a halt.

I couldn't make things right with Tio. I wouldn't know where to start. The swirling in my stomach whipped up as I thought about facing him and everyone at school today. After everything that had happened with Dodo last night, I'd completely forgotten about what lay ahead.

I decided to keep singing as the lift made its way down, to distract myself and make myself feel better. It was almost as if the louder I sang, the stronger I felt. *But only if no one is listening*, I reminded myself.

As the lift approached the ground floor, I dropped my voice back down to a low hum. I started slouching again, but I still felt a little of that lightness inside me.

I think a small smile may have even settled on my face. I was going to confront Tio and everyone at school head on. I still had no idea that anything was wrong with the world.

WEDNESDAY

8.11 a.m.

I walked towards the doors that led outside. As I approached the exit, I remembered coming home with Mum last night after seeing Dodo. We'd left her bundled up on her sofa, but when she'd rung later on, Mum thought she was at her office. Where was she now?

I pushed the doors open and stepped outside. The cold air rushed towards me and I felt glad of my coat, scarf and hat. That was my last normal thought, because before I'd even taken three steps, I stopped abruptly.

It hit me straight away.

The quiet.

It was too quiet. Not quiet in the way that means it's not as busy as usual. It was just quiet, quiet and more quiet. There was nothing else.

No cars. No buses on the road. No cyclists zipping past.

No one walking down the street. Not one single person.

No voices. No dogs barking. No music drifting in from elsewhere.

There was no noise.

There was no noise because I was the only person around.

I looked at the shops that were usually lit up and open, but the metal shutters were closed, making a line of gloomy grey rectangles. When I glanced up at the windows of the block of flats nearby, all the curtains were still pulled close.

There were also things I hadn't noticed before. A huge stack of cardboard on the pavement across the road, the arm-like streetlights that bent over the pavement, the power lines that zigzagged across the street like giant cobwebs.

The light was gentle and soft that morning, almost misty. There'd been a light frost and there were traces of frost sparkling on the pavement, crisping the blades of the grass in the tiny garden at the bottom of our building.

It struck me as quite beautiful, and for some reason it made me even more certain that something was wrong, because in that moment it felt like I was the only person in the world to see that frosty grass, those diamond sparkles.

But it can't just be me. And, as I thought that, I was engulfed in a cloud of loneliness – I felt smaller than I ever had in my whole life.

'Hello,' I called out into the silence. 'Is anyone there?' My voice suddenly felt scratchy in my throat and I tried to call louder. 'Hello!'

I listened out for someone, anyone, to answer me back. But all I heard was silence. I shook my head to clear my thoughts and scanned around the street again and again, searching for any sign of life. *It can't just be me out here*, I told myself again. *There's got to be someone else. It must be a weird moment and a bus will come steaming past in a minute and the day will roll on like normal.*

I strained to hear any of the usual street sounds but there

was nothing: just silence. But as I continued to listen I realized the silence wasn't complete. I could hear other sounds that I'd never thought to stop and listen out for before.

There was the wind making the leaves rustle. The air seemed to move around me as though it were alive, darting here, dashing there, whipping through the trees, round and round. And as it rustled the leaves, it made me think of water – the surge of the sea from far away. I watched the last few leaves trickle down from the branches and collect on the ground in little heaps.

A cluster of rubbish skittered along the road, also carried by the wind. It kept tapping against the tarmac before it was lifted into the air. My shoes crunched as they pressed down on the frosted blades of grass.

Suddenly, I could so clearly imagine telling Dodo about those little details. I could picture her standing next to me, taking it in: the wind rushing through the leaves, the tapping rhythm of the cluster of rubbish, the crunch of my shoes on the frost. But when I looked to the side, I was still all alone.

I willed myself to spot someone else and I realized I was holding my breath, as though another person might appear if I waited long enough. All I knew for sure was that I didn't want to take a step forward. I didn't want to enter this quiet, odd world; I didn't want to believe that this was really happening. And so I waited there, frozen, listening to the wind and hoping everything would go back to normal.

I don't know how long I stood there. But the cold snaked around me and I felt myself shiver. It was more than just the weather making me feel chilly; it was coming from the inside out.

I was about to turn back. In my mind, I was already in the

lift, riding all the way back up to my floor, racing into our flat
to find Mum.

But then I heard footsteps.

WEDNESDAY

8.21 a.m.

It was so quiet that I could hear every step as the person's shoes slapped against the ground behind me. I spun round. It had to be someone from my building. I wondered if it was the jogger I saw almost every day – a man who wears a fluorescent yellow T-shirt and whose face becomes more and more pained with every step he takes. Or the woman with the spotty dog who goes for a walk most mornings. Or someone from the family who'd just moved over from Thailand.

For a moment, I imagined it might be Mum, rushing out to work, in a bit of a flap that she'd slept later than usual. Maybe this was it, the weird silence was over and everything would go back to how it always was.

But I knew that wasn't true. All I could hear were those footsteps. There was still no traffic or the buzz of street noise. It was just one person.

As I turned, I saw him spot me, and his mouth fell open in disbelief.

'Ana, you're awake!'

It was Tio.

He looked happy to see me. Oddly happy, like he was about to hug me. His dark eyes seemed to glow a little.

'Are you okay?' he asked, ignoring the fact that I hadn't said a word. 'I thought . . . for a moment . . . that I might be the only one.'

'The only one?' I hadn't meant to answer him. I didn't want to talk to him at all. But the words left my mouth before I could stop them.

'The only one awake. I heard a noise from your flat through the walls this morning, but later I thought I'd imagined it . . .'

My face crinkled with confusion.

'But you're awake. It's not just me,' Tio continued. 'Have you checked on your mum?'

I turned instantly to look up at our block of flats. I suddenly ached to see Mum. I needed that safe, solid feeling that came from being close to her.

'What do you mean?' I said, again unable not to reply to him.

'Everyone's asleep,' Tio said simply. 'Everyone but you and me.'

'Asleep?' I echoed. My mind raced to try to understand what he was saying. I could hear his words and work out what they meant, but I couldn't accept them as the truth. He couldn't really mean that *everyone* was asleep, could he?

'Yes, and they won't wake up. I tried a few things but there's no waking them.'

'How do you know it's everyone?' I blurted out.

Tio simply stretched out his arms and we surveyed the silent world together. 'I checked on everyone in my family, and I've been searching the streets, but there's no one else around.'

'But you haven't seen anyone else, other than your family, asleep?' I asked.

'I've passed other people too – in cars and buses – and it's like they all fell asleep where they were. No one will wake up.'

'But how, why—?'

'I'm not sure what's happened,' Tio interrupted. 'Maybe there's something in the water that made them fall asleep . . .'

'But we've drunk the water too,' I said.

Tio looked like he wanted to disagree, but he didn't say anything.

'Who would do that?' I asked. 'Why would they do that?'

Tio started to speak but stopped himself. Then he shrugged and said, 'I don't know. I haven't worked that bit out.'

'I'd better go and check on Mum,' I said, turning away. I didn't want to talk about silly ideas that didn't make sense when something so awful was happening.

'I'll come with you,' Tio said, bounding to my side.

'You don't have to. You can just wait here.'

'No, it's best if we stick together,' he said firmly and with such purpose that I knew I wouldn't be able to stop him coming with me.

I turned back on myself, Tio walking alongside me. I tried to ignore the relief I felt that there was someone else with me, even though that person was Tio. For a moment, it felt a bit like the old days when we were friends. But then I remembered everything that had happened between us and the feeling vanished.

CASE #41029973876628

Case Holder Notes:

WEDNESDAY – 8.21 a.m.

Primary Subject and Companion Subject meet.
    Energy Connection low.

WEDNESDAY

8.32 a.m.

We rode up in silence, and nobody else stopped the lift to get in. Though everything I'd seen so far suggested Tio was right, I still couldn't believe we were the only ones awake.

I turned my key in our front door lock and took a deep breath. I imagined that when I went in I'd find Mum rushing to leave the flat, packing her bag, grabbing her keys, and everything would go back to normal. I pushed the door open and burst into the flat.

But it was just how I left it. My empty cereal bowl was still sitting on the side in the kitchen; the glass of water that I'd half-drunk beside it. Mum's bedroom door was still closed and I couldn't hear any sign of movement on the other side.

'I'll wait here,' Tio said and went to the window of our living room and peered out at the street. I looked down with him for a moment. Now I knew what had happened, I could sense the stillness outside, even from all the way up here. It made me think that our street could be a painting because there was no movement at all – everything was still.

I went to Mum's room and rushed towards the comforting mound of her, curled up under the duvet.

'Mum, something's happened,' I started to say, but as I reached for her I realized Tio was right. She hadn't stirred as I came in, and as I pulled her towards me now, she still didn't wake. She continued to breathe in and out in a heavy, rhythmic way.

'Mum! Mum!' My voice grew louder and louder but she still showed no signs of movement. I rolled her over so I could see her face. Her eyes stayed closed and her cheeks felt warm and soft like peaches that had been sitting in the sun. I felt better, as I could feel her warmth, but I couldn't ignore the panic that was rising inside me. I remembered how deeply asleep she'd been last night. She'd still woken up in an instant. I wished so hard that the same would happen now.

I gave her shoulder a gentle prod and then when she didn't stir, a harder shove. I pulled the curtains open and flicked on the bedroom light. I imagined how she might screw up her eyes as the light flooded in but her face remained peaceful and unmoving – she didn't react at all.

I tried again and again.

'Wake up, wake up, please wake up.' My voice rang out shrill and desperate. 'Please, please, please.' I tried everything to wake her and with each unsuccessful attempt, I felt myself growing ever more frantic.

'Mum, please wake up.' I don't know how many times I said it.

After a while I heard myself getting quieter. My voice shrank until it stopped and I could only hear my own breathing, which came fast and shallow in small, desperate gasps.

I darted out of Mum's bedroom and ran past Tio towards Mum's phone. It was back where I'd found it last night, plugged in for charging.

I grabbed the phone and dialled 999. My hands felt numb so

it was difficult to push the buttons, but finally I managed it. It rang and rang and no one picked up.

'I tried that too,' Tio said quietly. And just for that moment the sadness in his voice made me forget about my reluctance to talk to him properly. I knew he felt the same as I did and, in that instant, that made me feel closer to him.

I kept listening to the phone ringing out. I waited so long that the rings turned into a flat bleep and the line went dead.

Although I knew I couldn't wake her, I returned to Mum's bedroom and sat next to her. There was a photograph in a frame on her bedside table – a picture of Mum and Dodo from long ago. Dodo's just a toddler in it. They both have toothy grins and funny haircuts with wonky fringes.

Dodo.

Mum's mobile was still in my hand and I scrolled quickly through her numbers until I found Dodo's name.

I tapped the screen to call her, then pressed the phone to the side of my face so hard that it almost hurt.

The phone rang. And rang. Then I heard a click and felt myself breathe out in relief that Dodo had answered – she was there and she was awake. But in the next moment, it went through to voicemail.

Hi, it's Dolores. I can't get to the phone right now but please leave a message and I'll get back to you as soon as I can.

I called again and again, each time until the answerphone message played so I could hear her voice. I tried to ignore the heavy feeling of emptiness that was swamping me.

When I came out of Mum's room, Tio was standing there expectantly as though to say, *I told you so,* but instead he asked me softly, 'Are you all right?'

'No, of course not.' I was so worried that I felt stiff with it. The worry had burrowed into every one of my bones. But I didn't tell him that. Tio was like a stranger to me, I realized. He wasn't behaving like he did at school and I couldn't understand it. I tugged at the sleeves of my jumper. I briefly wondered if I was wearing it inside out because it felt wrong.

'What shall we do?' he said, looking down at the floor.

'I don't know,' I replied. But then I felt my mind whirring.

'I think we should go and look for other people who are awake. It can't just be us. It can't be.'

'Who else?' Tio asked.

But I didn't answer him. I'd noticed a square of paper just behind him on our doormat that I was pretty sure hadn't been there before. I tried to think whether I'd seen it that morning when I'd left, but I'd been preoccupied with trying to open the latch on the door quietly because Mum was sleeping. I must have missed it.

'Hold on,' I said and went to pick it up.

As soon as my fingers closed around it, I knew who it was from. It was a creamy, silky type of paper that I recognized immediately: it had been pulled from one of Dodo's notebooks.

'What's that?' I heard Tio behind me.

I unfolded the square and in Dodo's scratchy writing, I read:

I've got to hide something.

I'm being watched.

I'm going to take it to the

W

'What is that?' Tio asked again.

'It's a note,' I said. 'From my auntie.'

'Dodo,' he said. He knew Dodo from when we were friends. She sometimes used to take us both out. The last time had probably been only a little while ago, before school had broken up for the summer, but it felt like it had been much, much longer.

'She's in danger, I think.' I felt worry flood through me as I spoke. 'And she knows something about this.'

'What?'

'I'm not sure ... but I think Dodo knows something about what's going on.'

'What makes you think that?'

At first, I clammed up and couldn't speak. I didn't want to share it all with Tio. But then I looked over at him, at his wide, curious eyes. Behind him I could see out of the window to the buildings stretching out into the distance. If he really was the only other person who was awake in our city, or even the entire world, then I needed to be able to speak to him. Despite the way he'd been treating me, I would have to open up. I took a deep breath and told him about what had happened the day before. That there'd been something Dodo wanted to tell us when she rang in the middle of the night.

'Then this note,' I said. 'What is she hiding? I think she knows something about all this.'

'I wonder who she thinks is watching her,' Tio mused.

I turned automatically towards the window but there was nothing to see – only the still, unmoving morning.

'She's an insomniac,' I suddenly remembered.

'What's that?'

'It means you have trouble sleeping.' I said. 'If anyone's awake, she will be.'

'Have you tried calling her?'

'Yes – there's no answer. But I think she's somewhere out there. Maybe at the place she mentioned here.' I pointed to Dodo's words, then gripped the note tightly, the tips of my fingers turning white.

'What does that mean?' Tio said, pointing to the spiky line at the bottom of the note.

'I don't know,' I said. 'But I think if we can work out what it means then we'll find her. And hopefully find out what's happening.'

CASE #41029973876628

Case Holder Notes:

WEDNESDAY – 9.16 a.m.

Primary Subject and Companion Subject leave
Primary Subject Home.
　Walk to find Primary Subject Relative.
　See: Error Report #41029973876628
#1: Primary Subject Relative.

WEDNESDAY

9.22 a.m.

'I mean, what else could it be?' Tio walked along the edge of the pavement, balancing as though he were on a tightrope. 'If it's not something people ate or drank, what could it be? I know it's a strange idea but what else could have happened?'

We could have walked on the road, which was mostly empty except for the odd car or bus with a sleeping driver at the steering wheel. But something was stopping us. Part of me wondered if it was because we were still trying to cling on to anything that felt normal. We'd just left our building and set off down the main road in the direction of Dodo's flat. Though we couldn't make sense of her note, her home seemed as good a place as any to start our search.

The road should have been swarming with traffic – it was a really busy one and you'd normally only be able to cross at the traffic lights – but it was now mostly deserted and everything on it was still. Walking this way, we'd go past the road for our school – I was very familiar with the route, but today it felt like we were exploring a new land.

'What else could have happened?' Tio prodded again. He blew out a breath, making steam appear. Seeing how cold it was made me burrow down into my coat a little more.

'Well – it just makes no sense we weren't affected too,' I answered Tio.

'Maybe we have … what's that word … immune … immunity?'

'Maybe,' I answered sceptically. 'It's just weird that of all the people in the world, it's me … and you.' I said the last bit almost in a whisper. We still hadn't spoken about the fact that we weren't friends any more, that we were actually less than friends because of Tio's bullying. All the things he'd done recently had made me feel like I was shrinking away.

I shot a sideways glance at Tio, but he was looking elsewhere. I wasn't sure if he had heard me or if he felt like I did: how strange it was to be talking as though nothing had happened between us.

The wind whistled through the trees overhead and I was reminded once again that there was no one else here but him and me. I clung on to the hope that we would find Dodo awake, but the other possibility was never far from my mind: Tio might be the only other person who I would see awake today.

But Tio wasn't acting in the same way as he'd been at school. He hadn't said anything that had upset me or done anything at all that would make it seem like we weren't friends. It was confusing and almost more troubling than him being straightforwardly nasty to me, as he had been recently.

I took a deep breath. 'Ti—'

But before I could even finish saying his name, he'd turned to me with mingled excitement and fear in his face.

'There's someone else awake,' he said. 'Over there!'

Before I had time to answer him, he was shouting again: 'Down there! They just went down there. Come on!'

He pointed to an alley that led off the main street, on the

other side from us, and then broke into a run. I had to sprint to catch up with him. I could feel my heart beating frantically from the running, but also from this wild new hope that we weren't the only ones awake.

We ran down the empty street, then turned down the alley. With its high walls and overgrown shrubbery, it felt dark, narrow and cold. All I could hear were our footsteps. Tio's a bit shorter than me but he can run really fast and I struggled to keep up with him.

When we emerged from the alley, we ran past a series of buildings that were built so close together that their walls stretched up all round us. It felt like we were in a maze. As I ran, everything I passed went by in a blur, but I realized that I'd not been this way before and that I didn't know these streets. Tio continued to run even though I couldn't see anyone ahead of us. There was nothing to suggest someone was running away from us.

Finally, Tio came to a stop. He leaned over, panting.

I tried to speak but my breath was coming in ragged bursts. 'Where did they go?' I finally asked.

Tio looked ahead of us and then to one side of the street and then the other. His whole body seemed to sag and he made a sound. Something between a groan, a sigh and a cry.

'They've gone,' he said. He held his head in both hands so I couldn't see his eyes. I wondered if he was crying, because that was what I felt like doing. At any moment, hot tears could have poured down my cheeks.

It was worse somehow to have seen someone and lost them, than never to have seen anyone at all.

The buildings towered all around us. They were so close

together that they felt like they were closing in, so slowly that we couldn't see them actually moving, but they seemed to bear down on us more and more every minute.

I didn't know whether it was the dizziness from sprinting, the disappointment that we'd lost the person Tio had seen, or just being in this strange, claustrophobic place, but I suddenly felt nauseous and fearful. I looked around for something, for anything, or really, for someone who could bring me some comfort.

But like everywhere else, there was no sign of anyone.

CASE #41029973876628

Case Holder Notes:

WEDNESDAY – 9.33 a.m.

See: Error Report #41029973876628 #2: Primary
Subject + Companion Subject.
   Proximity Alert #41029973876628 #2.
   Activate Defensive Shield: Level Two.

WEDNESDAY

9.43 a.m.

'Are you sure you saw somebody?' I asked for about the hundredth time.

'Definitely,' Tio snapped back.

We were trailing around the buildings, trying to retrace our steps to the main street, but it felt like we were just going round and round in a loop.

'I think we've been this way before,' I said. I couldn't stop myself from panicking that we couldn't find our way back.

I couldn't ignore the queasiness that had been building in my stomach since the moment we'd run in this direction. My entire body ached, not unlike the time I'd had flu. I couldn't tell if I was really starting to feel unwell, if it was the disappointment that we'd not found whoever Tio had seen or if it was because we seemed to be lost.

Judging by his hunched shoulders, Tio didn't like being here either. We trudged on. Finally, we found a street that looked familiar. It was the one that led to the alley that would take us back to the main street. The sickness I'd felt began to dull.

I thought back to the moment when Tio said he'd spotted

someone. I tried to remember the scene exactly, but I hadn't even caught a glimpse of whoever it was.

'What did they look like?' I asked.

'I only saw them for a second, but I think they were grown up, or at least older than us. They were bigger than we are, anyway.'

'Why would they run from us? We're just a couple of kids,' I wondered out loud.

Tio shrugged his shoulders.

'It doesn't make any sense,' I said. 'Like everything else today.'

Then Tio noticed the entrance to the alley and we broke into a run. I felt lighter and lighter as we ran, and then we were out, back on the main street.

I took a breath and something inside me unknotted. The autumn sun broke through the clouds and I could feel its warmth. For a moment, I felt a shift and the queasy, aching feeling that I'd had before dropped away. But then almost as soon as it had stopped, the swirling, coiling feeling of unease that I'd felt all morning took hold again. We were back at the same spot on the main street – we'd made no progress and we'd lost the only other person who we'd seen awake.

'Shall we keep going?' Tio asked.

'Yes, definitely,' I said. I pictured Dodo's face on Mum's phone screen again, how scared she looked and the way her eyes had darted over her shoulder before she said, *Maybe it's not safe to talk here* ... and hung up. What had Dodo learned that could explain what was happening today?

'Are you ready?' Tio's voice jolted me back to reality.

'Yes, let's go,' I said. My legs still felt slightly wobbly so I walked on slowly.

As we approached the turning to our school, I thought

about everyone who should have been there, if this were a normal day. They would fill the grey playground with their shrieks and energy, but now they were silent and motionless in their beds.

The thought of Layla lost to this weird sleep punched me in the gut. She was always moving, always doing. Even on the occasions when I had seen her asleep. Once when I was staying over at her house, she'd sat bolt upright and muttered, 'Time to go, Mr Octopus' before collapsing back into a heap and thrashing her legs around as if she were swimming breaststroke. We'd laughed so hard about it the next day when I told her what she'd done. The memory upset me even more. I couldn't believe I'd fallen out with Layla and now she was lost to sleep too.

I thought about the last time I'd seen her awake. She was mouthing, 'I'm sorry,' her eyes seeming to grow bigger and bigger, the way they always do just before she starts crying.

'Layla,' I muttered to myself.

'What?' Tio said.

'I'm just thinking out loud. We're about to go past Layla's mum's flat. She was staying there last night. It's round the corner from school.'

'So?'

'I want to try to wake her,' I said.

Tio exhaled. It sounded not unlike a hiss. 'I thought you wanted to find Dodo.'

'I do, I still do. But while we're going past, I want to check on Layla. It's only down that road. And I think we should try the school too. If you and I are awake, then other kids could be. They might go to school as well. I want to try to wake up Layla, then we'll walk there together.'

'Do you really think other people are awake?' Tio asked, his voice filled with doubt.

'Some must be, we've already seen that person in the alley. We have to keep trying to wake people up and trying to find others who are already awake,' I said, glossing over Tio's doubtful words. It was the first time he'd said he didn't think we'd find others, and I didn't want to hear any more. 'And I have to see how Layla is,' I added.

'Right,' Tio said, but that one small word sounded so angry.

'Is that okay? You don't have to come with me ...'

'Where is it?' Again, each word came out snappy and short.

'It's just down there,' I said, pointing.

This time, Tio didn't even reply.

'Is there anyone that you want to try?'

'Let's just go,' he huffed. But then he added, 'She's going to be asleep anyway.'

'There must be other people awake, so why not her?' I said.

Again, Tio didn't reply.

He stomped away and I realized the other Tio was back, the one who enjoyed being mean to me. This morning it had been different. It wasn't exactly like before when we were friends, but I felt we were growing a bit closer. But now I could feel that coldness from him again and I couldn't help but shiver.

WEDNESDAY

10.02 a.m.

We didn't speak all the way to Layla's.

Layla and her mum have a ground-floor flat, so when I pressed the doorbell we could hear it echo through the other side of the door. There was no answer.

'I'm going to check round the back,' I said.

'What's the point? If they didn't answer the door they must be asleep.' Tio had jammed his hands into his pockets and he looked ready to storm off.

I ignored him and went to the gate by the side of the house. It led to the back garden. My fingers reached for the thick, heavy chain and padlock that looped around the gate.

'I can climb it,' I said, more to myself than to Tio. 'Layla and I have done it before.'

I made it sound like we'd done it loads of times, but actually it had just been once and only Layla had managed it.

The gate shook slightly as I pulled myself up, but I found a curl of wrought iron to use as a foothold. I reached up my hand to another curl, but the metal dug into my palm and I almost slipped off entirely.

I held Layla's face in my mind, remembering how she'd looked at me yesterday, as I reached for a higher part of the gate so I could pull myself up.

When I got to the top, I swung myself over, trying not to look down and see how far I was from the ground.

'There,' I said when I landed on the other side of the gate. 'Your turn. If you're coming, that is.'

Tio grumbled something I didn't hear but began his climb. He was much faster than me and jumped off the gate on the other side in no time, landing with a loud thud.

The garden was frosted over and some of the plants were silvery, while others had collapsed into a grey-green mulch. Layla's bedroom was at the back of the house and had doors that opened directly out to the garden. I ran over to them and tried to peer through a crack in the curtains, pressing my nose up against the glass.

'I can see her,' I said, although all I could make out was her thin arm on top of the duvet. But somehow being so close to her made me feel a little better. 'Layla!' I knocked on the door so hard that the glass rattled in its frame.

'I told you,' Tio muttered. 'Everyone's asleep.'

'I have to check on the people who ...' But I didn't finish the sentence, because I'd been going to say, 'mean something to me'.

'You didn't have to come with me, you know,' I snapped instead.

'I said I would, didn't I?' Tio said back.

Hot anger flooded through my body. Part of me wished that he wasn't with me. I knew that he didn't really want to be here – something had changed since we'd first met this morning – but there was another part of me that didn't want to be alone, who would take his grumpy company over being in this quiet place on my own.

'Layla!' I tried again and thumped the door.

I pressed my face to the glass and kept my eyes glued to her arm. I willed it to move and for Layla to sit up, rub her eyes and then look over at me. I could so easily imagine her face moving and her mouth opening, shocked that I was standing outside her window. And then once she'd learned what had happened, she'd know what to do straight away. She'd think of a plan.

But her arm didn't move a millimetre.

WEDNESDAY

10.18 a.m.

After climbing back over the gate, we turned in the direction of school. Neither of us spoke but I could feel smugness coming off Tio in waves. He didn't need to say *I told you so* for me to know he was thinking it. It was like he was glad we'd found Layla sleeping like everyone else.

As we approached the school building, it was as quiet as everything else around it. The gates were closed and though we tried every entrance, none of them were open. Once again, I could sense Tio's disapproval of my plan, although he didn't actually say anything. It was all in the stiff way he was holding his body and the small, frustrated sighs he kept letting out.

'Let's leave a note,' I suggested. 'Just in case someone comes along.'

I rummaged in my rucksack to find a scrap of paper and a pen, and then leaned on the hard, brick wall to write: *Ana and Tio from Year Six have been here. If you're awake too, let us know.*

'How are they going to do that?' Tio asked. I felt sure he thought this idea was silly as well.

'Your phone,' I said. I didn't have one because Mum said I had to wait until I was older, but Tio was one of the first in our year to get one. 'What's your number?'

'I haven't got it. It went through the wash again.'

I crossed out the last sentence and thought for a moment.

'What if we put that we'll come back at a certain time to meet anyone else who sees the note.'

'Yes, okay.' Tio said shortly. Since we'd been to Layla's, this was the most that we'd spoken.

'What time is it now?' I asked.

'Almost half past ten,' Tio said after glancing at his watch.

'So, if I say one o'clock, that should give us time to walk to Dodo's and then come back.' Tio nodded briefly in agreement.

I leaned against the wall again and wrote: *We'll come back at one p.m. – if you're awake too, come here to meet us at that time.* I managed to tuck the note just behind the metal buzzer by folding the bottom of the paper so it was wedged right in. I tested it a few times to make sure it wouldn't slip out and fly away.

'It's going to be all right, isn't it?' Tio suddenly blurted out. 'It won't be like this . . . for ever.'

'Of course not,' I replied. 'I'm sure we'll find some other people. We saw one already, didn't we? And then we'll work out how to wake everyone else up. It's probably something quite simple. Maybe by the time we come back here, there'll be others waiting to see us. Maybe Layla will have woken up. Maybe she'll be here too.'

I knew I was speaking too quickly and too loudly. I was trying to convince myself everything would be all right, but the truth was that I didn't really believe it would.

WEDNESDAY

10.43 a.m.

I'd only ever been to Dodo's on the bus, but I knew the way because I always looked out of the bus windows. You had to go down the main street for quite a long time, then when you got to a big intersection, you turned right and then right again.

It could take about ten minutes on the bus from our flat, or twenty if the traffic was really bad. I wasn't sure how long it would take us to walk there from where we were, so I tried to set a quick pace, just in case time would be tight to make it back to school for one.

I was walking faster than Tio, always just a little bit ahead of him.

'It's quite far down this road,' I said, trying to encourage him to speed up. I felt my legs straining, wanting to break into a run. Now we were heading towards Dodo's flat, I couldn't get there fast enough. I felt certain that Dodo would be awake. I really needed her to be. We had to get to the bottom of what was happening and I had no idea where else to look for answers.

Tio nodded, but he didn't walk any faster. If anything, I thought I heard his footsteps drag a little more against the pavement.

Since we'd left the school, he'd fallen into an even worse mood than when we were at Layla's. He'd stopped talking to me, just grunting in agreement whenever I asked him a question. It felt like I was having to lug him around with me, along with my fears about what was going on today.

As he slowed down even more, annoyance prickled through me. I was sick with worry too, but we had to keep going. I looked forward. The road stretched on and on in front of us – there was still so much ground to cover. Then I looked back again at Tio, who was taking even smaller steps now, and I felt the prickles turn to something bigger. Frustration rose inside me.

'Look,' I said, stopping and turning around. 'I know you don't want to come with me ...'

'Dodo's not going to be awake,' Tio said – so quickly and sharply, it felt like a slap.

'She might be,' I replied, although I could hear the slight wobble in my voice.

'It just seems maybe a bit much to go all this way. If she was awake, then don't you think she would have contacted you?' There was a hardness in Tio's voice that I recognized from school.

I tried to take a breath to answer, but it caught in my throat. I remembered again how confused Dodo had been about losing a chunk of Monday, and that no one could really explain it. What if something worse had happened and she'd lost even more of her memory?

'I don't think she'd be able to, actually,' I tried to reply but my voice wavered and I couldn't speak clearly. I swallowed hard and looked Tio straight in the eye. I refused to be intimidated by him. 'Last night, Dodo's memory was all over the place. She'd forgotten things that we do every week, and some of what she'd done during the day, too. Something was wrong with her memory. That's why it's even more important that I go and see her.'

Tio huffed in response. Clearly he didn't feel like using words right now.

We fell into silence again. Then Tio kicked at the ground. He looked like he was going to turn round and take off and it reminded me of how he and Chidi had pranced down the corridors as they mocked me. The horrible, churning loneliness I'd felt came back now, all mixed up with embarrassment and fear.

I'd been too worried at first to notice that Tio had seemed different this morning, and now I realized that he wasn't anyway.

'I overheard you on Monday,' I said suddenly. 'When you came back upstairs I was in the classroom. I heard you and Chidi making fun of me.'

Tio looked down at his feet.

'You've been making fun of me for a while now. You knew how much it would hurt.' Now I was talking about it, everything came spilling out of me. All the upset that had been gradually wearing me down was coursing through me, urging me to speak.

Something that had been building for a long time finally slotted into place as I said those words. We didn't know each other any more.

'You don't like me,' I said. 'I get it. We're not friends any more. We don't have to spend time together just because of what's happening today, do we?'

As I said that, I realized I meant it. Though I was frightened by the thought of being alone, I could do this myself. I didn't need to stay with him just because I felt scared of being on my own today.

Tio kept his head down. He didn't answer me.

I'd thought silence couldn't be loud, but now it felt like a roaring in my ears. I waited for Tio to say something, but he didn't speak. The roaring grew louder and louder, filling my head. Red-hot rage spiked through me. I couldn't believe he wasn't speaking to me, and more than that, I realized how furious I was that he'd been treating me badly. Now I'd faced up to how upset and ashamed he'd made me feel, all that was left was a storming rage.

'You can't even defend yourself now,' I spat. 'Now that I'm standing up to you, you can't even look me in the eye.'

My voice trembled. I was so furious with him that I could feel my anger swinging like a heavy pendulum through me.

'I don't need you,' I said. 'I don't need you in my life. I have the best friend in the world . . .' But Tio interrupted my tirade by looking up sharply and his cold eyes finally met mine.

'You've got no one else today, though, have you? Where's your Layla now?' He taunted.

I floundered for just a moment.

'Asleep and useless and *stupid*,' he said angrily.

'She's more to me asleep than you are awake,' I said. I thought Tio's eyes flickered for just a moment as though my words had stung him, but then in the next he was full of confidence.

'You're right, we don't have to spend time together just because of today. I don't want to be with you for another minute.'

'Well, that's good because I don't want to be with you either,' I said, although hearing him say that made me feel hollow and empty, and I was even more aware of how lonely I felt.

'Good,' Tio answered back.

There was a moment when it seemed we both might stomp

off. I felt blood surging through my ears, and I was whipped up and angry, as if the storm inside me was full-blown, raging and thundering with no end in sight. But we didn't walk away from each other. We both stayed exactly where we were for just a beat longer.

Then Tio kicked at the ground again, and the sound pulled a trigger inside me. I didn't want to be around him for a moment longer. I spun round and walked off in the direction of Dodo's, stamping along the road as though I could inject my anger into the tarmac.

CASE #41029973876628

Case Holder Notes:

WEDNESDAY – 11.05 a.m.

Primary Subject and Companion Subject separate.
   Energy Tension high.
   Energy Connection extremely low.
   Initiate countdown to Case termination.

WEDNESDAY

11.05 a.m.

I walked quickly, trying to concentrate on the beat of my footsteps on the road. I fixed my gaze upon the thickly painted white lines that reached out endlessly in front of me, but I kept replaying what had just happened with Tio over and over again.

I don't want to be with you for another minute. His voice rang through my head, and I was back to that same empty feeling I'd had when he'd spat the words at me. Though I knew it shouldn't have been a surprise after everything that had been happening at school, I hadn't realized until this moment that a tiny part of me still wondered if Tio and I might become friends again.

Perhaps that hope had grown today, ever since that moment when he came running towards me this morning. He'd seemed different to how he'd been at school recently, more like the old Tio, more like a friend. But then, I asked myself, was that just because I was the only other person in the world he could talk to right now?

I felt my breath grow short and ragged as I kept thinking it all through. A tightness gnawed at my chest. I felt overwhelmed.

What had I done? Had I really just walked away from the only other person who was awake?

The urge to look behind me to check that he was still there was too strong. It might not be too late. But when I looked back, I saw that he was gone.

I kept marching down the road, all the time straining to hear any sounds of people.

As soon as I realized that Tio had left, I felt a huge pang of loneliness. But as I stopped there, so completely by myself, something else stirred within me.

I could work out what was happening on my own. I still had a plan of action: I had to find Dodo. Surely she'd be at her flat, or there'd be a clue there about where she was. I could figure it out from there.

As I set off again in the direction of Dodo's flat, I started to feel a little better. With each step, I felt a bit stronger and more resolved that I could do this on my own. My anger with Tio began to fade and was replaced with a little seed of hope that maybe things would still be okay if I found Dodo.

At times, I thought I could sense something moving and I'd whirl around to see what it was. I might spot an old plastic bag that was blowing across the road, or leaves falling from a tree branch, but that was all.

The thin mist continued to linger in the air and the late-morning light coated everything with a warm feeling, although I still needed to rub my hands together to stop them from getting too cold.

I came across a tree that had branches clustered with berries and my head jerked up as I spotted a blackbird flitting from twig to twig, plucking them as it went. I spun around and I realized as I was doing it that I was looking for Tio, wanting more than anything to share this moment with him and tell him the thoughts that were racing through my mind. Birds were awake. It was not just Tio and me. There was the blackbird too, and as though they understood that I was looking for them, I saw a pair of seagulls glide through the mist high above me.

I wondered if other animals were awake too, and I thought of all the pets that might be waiting for their owners to wake up, waiting for breakfast, a stroke or a walk. I wondered if we would hear them if we thoroughly searched a building. For a few moments, I pictured us, Tio and me, going from house to house, pressing our ears to each front door, listening for any dogs or cats or rabbits trapped inside. We could collect them all together to make a pack. But as I remembered our last conversation, the image dissolved away.

I watched the blackbird for a few more moments and felt glad for it as it flew away. It was free, free to fly and look for food – free just to be.

It had no idea what was going on.

WEDNESDAY

11.39 a.m.

As I kept walking, though I tried to block it out, a question kept floating around in my mind: *Should I return to school at one o'clock to see if I can find Tio?*

From the moment I saw that he'd gone, a big part of me had wanted to go back to school to find him. Despite things being so awful between us, I wanted us to help each other today.

But what if he didn't go back there? Maybe he'd found other people awake, perhaps even his friends from school. He wouldn't come back and find me then.

The thoughts fizzed through my brain, feeling like they were leaving wormholes trailing behind them.

It was only as I came to a large traffic intersection, which I recognized as the one close to Dodo's, that I could push the thought of Tio from my mind. I broke into a run and weaved through the trees until I reached Dodo's building.

The outside door hadn't been closed properly. There was a problem with the latch – I'd heard Dodo complaining about it to Mum, but now I was glad that it hadn't been fixed so I could get in. I took the stairs two at a time. The hallway was empty, and like everywhere else I'd been, there was a quiet that convinced me no one here was awake.

I sped up as Dodo's front door came into view. The entrance to her flat is at the end of the hallway, and there's a little corner outside her door where she has lots of flowerpots. Dodo calls it 'her garden', which always makes Mum laugh. In the summer it would be a mass of red, but now the stalks looked like gnarly fingers growing out of the pots. I beat my fist against the door and pushed the letterbox open so I could peer through.

Nothing. No answer.

But what if Dodo couldn't get out of her bed? What if she'd gotten worse since we saw her last night? I couldn't, *wouldn't*, let go of the hope that she might still be awake. I started to lift up the flowerpots, one after the other. I'd overheard Mum telling Jenna last night that Dodo hid a spare key under one of them for emergencies. But what if it hadn't been put back last night? I lost count of how many pots I lifted, and I was almost sure that the spare key must still be in Dodo's flat, when I glimpsed a dull, brass key. I grasped it tightly. I felt like whooping aloud – finally, something was going right.

I pushed the key into the lock, swung the door open and shouted as loudly as I could, 'Dodo! It's me! It's Ana!'

I rushed through the flat, past the living room and down towards her bedroom. As I ran, I noticed an assortment of odd details that I tried to piece together to make sense. All they really made clear, though, was that Dodo wasn't awake. She wasn't in the living room. Instead, her blue cardigan was flung across the sofa – it looked like a creature taking a rest, stretched out asleep. There wasn't any sound coming from the kitchen, not a kettle whistling nor a tap running. The empty mug and plate of crumbs from Dodo's toast the night before were still on the coffee table, untouched.

I sped up but as I got closer to the bedroom, I knew something was very wrong before I even got there.

The door was ajar, and through the gap I could see her bed. The bedclothes had been stripped and her duvet was in a tangle on the floor.

Fear crawled down my back like a spider. Then a wave of panic rose up inside me as I took it all in. There was no sign of Dodo – not awake or asleep.

WEDNESDAY

12.06 p.m.

There was no reason to stay there, but I found myself sinking down onto Dodo's bed. Like before, after the worry that I didn't know where she was had set in, I was left deflated, exhausted by the wave of emotions that kept washing around inside me today.

I reached into my pocket and pulled out the note Dodo had written to me. It already felt soft and crinkled because I'd read it so many times. I carefully unfolded it, then smoothed it out on my lap and traced my fingers over the words as I read them again: *I've got to hide something. I'm being watched. I'm going to take it to the . . .* and then came that funny zigzag line.

I scanned every part of the bedroom in case I could spot a similar zigzag. But I could see nothing.

Instead, familiar faces smiled down at me from the walls: Dodo had pinned photos all over her bedroom. There were lots of recent ones of her with Mum and me, and pictures of her and her best friend, Karen, from a big trip to South America they went on last year. They were laughing in one of them, with giant leaves framing their faces like lions' manes. But Dodo also had old photos up. There were some of me from when I was a toddler, and there was the same one I saw in Mum's room from when they were little. Among the people, there were photographs of plants and animals and drawings she'd done: towering sequoia trees, fox cubs, shaggy-looking mushrooms and beautiful butterflies. Maybe that was why I thought her bedroom looked a bit like a forest – not one of trees, but a forest full of people and creatures.

I noticed a small palette of watercolour paints by the side of Dodo's bed. They were next to a glass of murky-looking water that had a paintbrush in it. There were a few cylinders of oil pastel paints in a box, too. The black one had been used so much that it looked like nothing else could be squeezed out of it. I also spotted a book with pictures of bees on the front, peeping out from under the bed.

Drawers had been left half-open and her wardrobe doors weren't properly closed. It seemed like she'd been searching for something. Or packing up to go away in a rush, like she hadn't had any warning.

I tried to figure out if anything was missing, but couldn't be sure. All I could see was what was still there: her dressing gown hanging on the back of the door and the bedding that looked like it had been pulled from the mattress in one big sweep.

I was reluctant to leave her bedroom. It felt safe in there. I liked to be close to the photos that Dodo had on her wall, because they made me forget for a small sliver of a moment that I was all alone. I could block out what was happening. But I smoothed down the note from Dodo once more and forced myself to go and look round the rest of the flat. I had to see if I could find any clues to where Dodo might be, and if I could spot anything that would show me what that zigzag line on the note meant.

But I didn't find anything in the living room or in the small, crowded kitchen. I looked at all the scraps of paper that were stuck on the fridge with magnets, and at the calendar hanging on the wall, but I couldn't understand most of the notes that were on it – Dodo had written in scribbles, and I could only decipher one of them: when my school concert was. She had drawn little dashes all around it. *Ana's Stars Concert*, it read. There was no sign of the zigzag line from the note.

Like in her bedroom, some things here were a little out of place after Mum and I had been round the night before. Some of the cushions that were meant to be on the sofa were on the floor as if they'd been thrown there. Dodo often has piles of books around the flat, but they felt a little more disorganized than I remembered. The bin in the kitchen was sitting at an angle, not neatly against the wall as it usually was.

All this gave me the impression that Dodo had been packing in a hurry or looking for something. Then I had a thought that stopped me dead: *What if it wasn't Dodo looking for something? What if it was someone else?* I looked at her note again: *I'm being watched*, it said. What if the people watching her had raided her flat?

My brain scrambled for answers but of course it found none, only more and more questions. Why was Dodo being watched? Who was doing it? If the same person or people had been searching her flat, what were they looking for? And had they found Dodo? Was that why she wasn't here?

I retreated into Dodo's bedroom and pressed a hand into her pillow. It bounced back into shape softly as I looked around the room once more. Glancing again at her bedside table – at the watercolour paints, the pastels and the pot of clouded water – I wondered if I'd missed anything. A clue that would unlock the meaning of her note or a sign that would tell me where she might be.

That was when I spotted it.

Her notebook, the one she'd shown me the night before, was slotted between her bed and the table. The space was the perfect size for it, but the notebook was so neatly tucked away there that I might not have noticed it if my gaze hadn't wandered from the bedside table. I reached for the angular, black cover and pulled it towards me.

I knew immediately that there was something different about it, but I couldn't tell what by looking at the outside.

I opened it up and flicked past the pages of foxes that Dodo had drawn, the 'Vulpes vulpes' as she called them, then I came to the pages where the drawings of the funny-looking creature from her dreams should have been.

The paper had been torn from the spine of the notebook. Jagged paper edges were the only sign that the pages once existed. That was why the notebook felt different – it was lighter because so many pages had been ripped out.

There wasn't a single drawing of the creature left in the book.

WEDNESDAY

12.17 p.m.

I ran my finger over the torn edges of the notebook paper and tried to remember every detail that Dodo had told me about those creatures. I was able to vividly imagine them, but I still felt no closer to understanding what they had to do with anything. Why had the drawings of them been ripped out? Had Dodo done that?

I looked through the bin in her bedroom but found nothing apart from balled-up tissues and old receipts. Next, I peered into the kitchen bin, which looked like it had been moved, and poked around in the rubbish, but the drawings weren't in there either.

In my mind, I went through everything I'd learned since I'd got there.

Dodo isn't here.

It looks like Dodo was packing to go away in a hurry. Or maybe Dodo, or someone else, was searching for something.

The drawings of the weird creature have been torn out of her notebook, and there's no sign of them anywhere. I don't know who did that – Dodo, or again, it might have been someone else.

It felt like one of the jigsaw puzzles we'd started doing on

Chewy Tuesdays before we realized that we were no good at them. I was sure all the information fitted together somehow, but I couldn't figure it out.

I glanced at the clock on Dodo's kitchen wall, then jumped a little – it was already twenty past twelve! It had taken me about an hour to walk here, but Tio had been walking slowly and we'd had an argument. I totted up the numbers and thought it would take me about forty-five minutes to get back to school, if I went quickly. I'd spent longer here than I'd planned, so I'd really need to rush if I was going to make it by one o'clock.

I looked around Dodo's flat one more time and had the familiar sense that I was failing to spot something, though I knew that I had to leave now or risk missing Tio. That's if he actually turned up, of course.

I left the flat reluctantly, hiding the key under the flowerpot where I'd found it.

I was almost back on the road and about to step onto the pavement when a coffee cup rolled in front of me. It came to a stop next to an old takeaway bag that had been crushed into a ball. A memory from last night resurfaced at the sight of the scrunched-up paper. Dodo had ripped one of the pages of the notebook out. I don't know why I hadn't remembered it before, but now here it was, as sharp as the cold autumn's light.

She'd said something like, 'That shouldn't be in here' as she did it. So maybe she was the one who had torn out the other sketches, too. But the part of the memory that had me sprinting back towards Dodo's front door was that she'd screwed that sketch up into a tight ball in her hand. Then she'd buried it deep inside one of the long pockets of her hairy blue cardigan. The cardigan that had been lying across the sofa like a cat just now.

I raced back to her flat, jamming the key into her front door, and almost stumbled into the living room.

I dug my hand into the pockets of the cardigan and my fingers closed around a balled-up piece of paper. For the first time that day, I felt relief, but just behind it my curiosity was prickling and all the questions that had been rushing through my mind before came back, even sharper and more jagged now.

The drawing was just as I had remembered it. Heavy black lines, etched deeply into the paper, made up the creature's shadowy shape. Several tentacles that looked similar to elephant trunks or octopus limbs wound out from its body. It had no face, but I felt as if it were somehow peering out at me nonetheless.

I remembered Dodo saying she thought it came from a dream she'd had. As I traced my fingers over the picture, fear sliced through me and along with it came even more questions for which I had no answers. What was this thing? Why had Dodo seen it in a dream? And then the one that made me feel sick: did this creature exist somewhere in the real world?

My eyes slid to Dodo's living-room window and the view of bare trees and the empty communal garden. Imagining this shadowy thing stalking across the flowerbeds scared me so much that I tried to squash the thought as soon as it arrived. But I knew I wouldn't be able to stop myself imagining it over and over again.

I folded up the drawing carefully, smoothing down the creases and, although I wanted to look at it for longer, I tucked it into my pocket and sped away from Dodo's flat once more.

Back on the silent main street, all I could think about was whether that creature had anything to with Dodo's disappearance. My eyes were constantly flickering towards any shadows I passed, in case it might really be out here somewhere.

I swivelled round at the thought. There was no one beside me, of course, but I couldn't dismiss the uncanny feeling that I wasn't alone, that maybe I was being watched. But every time I stopped to look, there was nothing to see.

I tried to brush off my fears and walked along quickly, trying not to question the world that was beginning to feel more normal to me now: the cars frozen on the roads, the closed-up shops, the absence of anyone else.

The morning had now lost its hazy promise, the sky having turned an impenetrable grey-white colour. I wondered if it would start raining, and the chill in the air made me hurry along.

CASE #41029973876628

Case Holder Notes:

WEDNESDAY – 12.56 p.m.

Primary Subject looks all around her.
   Energy Tension high.

WEDNESDAY

1.10 p.m.

I ran past a secondary school and glanced up to check the clock on the side of the building – ten past one. I tried to speed up, but my legs wouldn't carry me any faster.

'Almost there, almost there,' I said to myself. My voice came out taut – I realized I was pleading with someone, something, myself – for me to be on time, for Tio to be waiting for me.

It felt hard to breathe as I pushed on, running as hard as I could towards my school. I could make out the top of the roof in the distance, then I turned down the road to where the entrance was, my eyes fixed upon the gate, where we had left the note.

Nobody was there.

I still ran all the rest of the way as though that might make some difference.

Breathless, I reached the gate and immediately spotted that the note was gone. I scanned everywhere for another one – perhaps Tio had been there and left me a note when I didn't show up. One that told me where I could find him.

But there was nothing. No note.

'He's not here,' I tried to say, but my voice gave way. My breath

113

was still coming in ragged bursts and it finally hit me that Tio wasn't there.

It felt like something inside me collapsed in that moment, as though an invisible string holding me up had been slashed. My body sank to the ground, my back pressed up against the school gate.

That was when I spotted him.

Sitting on one of the walls opposite the entrance, leaning against a stone pillar, was Tio. He wasn't swinging his legs or scuffing his shoes against the bricks the way I'd seen him do so many times before. He was absolutely still.

'Tio!' I shouted when I saw him. My voice rang out across the road. I saw a couple of crows on the road take off in surprise, but he didn't turn towards me.

I sprang to my feet, running across the road in a desperate race to get to him. I felt a heavy lump in my throat form as I took him in – he was sat leaning against the stone of the pillar, his eyes closed: asleep.

CASE #41029973876628

Case Holder Notes:

WEDNESDAY – 1.22 p.m.

Primary Subject and Companion Subject
(in rest state) reunite.

WEDNESDAY

1.22 p.m.

Without thinking, I grabbed Tio by the jacket and shook him as hard as I could. 'Don't be asleep, don't be asleep,' I heard myself shouting over and over.

It wasn't quite like how it was with Mum. I can't explain exactly why, but he didn't seem as deeply asleep as she had been. Maybe his body didn't feel quite as heavy or maybe his eyelids gave the smallest of flickers, but as I shook him I was certain that I could wake him, if I just kept going.

I had to really, really want to wake him up.

Nothing happened at first, but then his eyes opened for a second and closed just as quickly. Then his mouth twitched, the motion almost imperceptible, but he had definitely moved.

'Tio! Tio!' I shouted. At the sound of his name, his eyes opened and he blinked rapidly. They locked with mine and he looked panicked and afraid. He opened his mouth to speak but no sound came out. Then his eyes closed again and his mouth went slack.

'Tio! Tio! Tio!' It sounded like an alarm going off – my voice blaring out at full volume. I couldn't let him stay asleep, I knew that with absolute certainty. Everything else that had happened between us – the argument and what had been happening at

116

school – faded away. All I felt was a desperate hope that he would wake up alongside a black hole of worry that he might not. His eyes fluttered open again and I pressed my hand to his cheek. This time he looked more awake, and as he came to, the fear had vanished from his eyes.

'Ana,' he muttered groggily. 'What … where … ?'

'You were asleep.' I rushed to fill in the blanks. 'I thought you might not wake up. Like the others.'

He sat up straight and rubbed his eyes furiously. Then he stared into the distance, still blinking.

'Me too,' he said. 'I didn't think that I would wake up either.'

That black hole of despair that I'd felt before, where I'd worried that he wouldn't wake up, I still felt it inside me. Because now I was sure that whatever had happened between us, I couldn't lose Tio too. I needed him to be awake and with me and if he wasn't, I knew I would be completely lost.

CASE #41029973876628

Case Holder Notes:

WEDNESDAY – 1.25 p.m.

Companion Subject awoken by Primary Subject.
   See: Connection Report #41029973876628
#1: Primary Subject = Companion Subject.
   Case #41029973876628 continues.

WEDNESDAY

1.27 p.m.

'I was sitting waiting for you and then I leaned against the side of the pillar for just a moment. I thought, *Oh, I feel a little bit tired* and that was it. I didn't mean to fall asleep – I closed my eyes and I was gone.

'But it must have happened just before you came, I think. Because I could hear you saying something. I tried to open my eyes, but it was like ... like the lids were glued together. I was trying to wake up but something was stopping me, something was making me stay asleep. Then you started shouting and that helped a bit. I could see your face in little snatches, and I knew that if I didn't make a big effort to wake up, I would be like everyone else and you wouldn't be able to wake me. It was like I was trapped underwater, trying to swim upwards, really having to kick to be able to get back to the surface.'

At that, he took a deep breath. It was the first time he'd stopped talking since he woke up, when I'd yelled, 'What happened? What happened?' at him.

'I wonder what it was that made you go to sleep like that,' I pondered. 'Why the sleep stuff is affecting you now.'

I managed to keep my voice steady, but on the inside I felt all over the place. I'd so very nearly ended up being the only person awake, and the thought terrified me. If I hadn't woken Tio, then I would be completely alone. It made me feel very, very small and I could still sense that black hole inside me.

Tio nodded. He blinked again, then widened his eyes as though to reassure himself that he really was awake.

'You know, I thought you weren't coming,' Tio said quietly. I couldn't read his expression.

'I . . . I didn't mean to be so late,' I admitted. 'It just took longer than I thought . . . and then . . .' My voice trailed off. I didn't want to admit I was worried that someone had been watching me.

'It was kind of . . . scary . . . being alone,' Tio said in a small voice.

'It was,' I agreed quickly. 'It feels . . . empty not seeing people. Even the people you don't know very well but you see all the time. Not to mention our families and . . . everyone at school.' I was about to say friends but couldn't manage it because of the weirdness between us. We had been friends and now I didn't know what we were.

'So no one else turned up,' Tio said. 'But the note has gone.'

'I thought you took it.' My mind swam with possibilities of what might have happened to it, but I couldn't make sense of any of it.

'Must have been blown away,' he said.

'Or someone else took it?' I suggested hopefully.

Then why would they have taken it? Wouldn't they have just left it for more people to see?' Tio answered.

'I-I just . . .'

'I know,' Tio said. 'You want there to be more people awake than just you and me.'

I tried to answer but the words caught in my throat because he was right. He was the last person in the world I'd have chosen to share this situation with me. I remembered him laughing at me on the stage in the hall, overhearing his taunting voice in the corridor, the way he'd spoken to me earlier today before I left to go to Dodo's.

As though he knew what I was thinking, Tio looked at the pavement and started to speak. 'Ana, I'm sorry – about everything.'

I glanced up at him sharply. He wasn't looking down at the ground any more. Instead, he met my eye.

'I shouldn't have done those things. I didn't ... want to but I just ...'

'You did them,' I replied slowly. I could feel a huge lump throbbing in my chest as though my heart actually hurt as I remembered everything he'd done to me.

'I've been thinking it over since you walked off,' Tio said. 'You're right – we're not friends any more. Ever since Layla started—'

'Layla? What's Layla got to do with it?' I interrupted.

Tio took a deep breath. 'Since Layla started at our school, I thought you were the one who didn't want to be friends with me.'

'What? That doesn't make sense. What have I ever done to make you think that?' I asked.

'You were always busy – you were always with Layla,' Tio muttered, looking at the ground again.

'But so were you – you've got loads of other friends! Kwame and Della and Chidi—' I blustered.

'Think about it – I only got closer to them since Layla joined – when you stopped hanging out with me,' Tio said to the ground.

'I didn't...' I started to say, but I began to think about the last few months, seeing my memories with fresh eyes. At the end of the last school year, our teacher had asked me and a few other students to buddy up with Layla because she arrived so late in the year. Since then, Layla and I had become inseparable. Had I really not made any time for Tio?

I couldn't work out what had happened first: me not spending time with Tio because Layla was there, or me not wanting to spend time with Tio because of the way he was acting.

'I thought it would get better,' Tio said. 'Maybe Layla would move schools again and it would go back to how things were before she arrived. But it's just got worse and worse. And Layla hates me—'

'She doesn't hate you,' I interrupted, although the words came out sounding uncertain.

'She does,' Tio said vehemently. 'Since you became friends...'

I grappled to make sense of what Tio was saying.

'Let me get this right, you were just being mean to me because you thought I didn't like you any more?'

Tio gave a tiny nod and then looked away.

'That's so stupid,' I said, then couldn't stop myself from adding, 'and I don't get why you were so horrible to me. You made me feel so awful about myself, about how bad my singing is and...'

'But it's so obvious that you're not a bad singer. I just got angry that you were going to sing at the concert, knowing everyone would be looking at you and telling you how good you were afterwards. I'm not good at anything.'

'What?' I said, still trying to piece together everything that Tio was saying. I felt a dull ache in my brain from trying to process this new information. I looked at Tio with suspicion. Did I really believe what he was telling me?

'Even my mum thinks it,' Tio said.

'What are you talking about?' I asked.

'I heard her one day talking about us kids – that Denise was so good with books and Sami's so athletic and Rita's the kind one ... but she didn't say *anything* about me.'

'That doesn't mean anything,' I said quickly. 'You probably just didn't hear the bit where she was talking about you.'

'But I know it too,' Tio said. 'That I'm not that good at anything.'

You were good at being mean to me, I thought but I stopped myself from saying it out loud. I looked at Tio, whose eyes were still fixed on the ground and, in that moment, he reminded me of the friend I'd used to know. I took a deep breath.

'Sometimes,' I said, remembering something Layla would say, that her mum would tell her, 'We can get so worried about being good at something that we don't think about what we actually enjoy. What do you enjoy doing?'

'Enjoy? I don't know. I mean ... I like music too. Remember when we had that music teacher last year and we did a few drumming classes. And then only a few people got picked to do it every week after that?' Tio said.

'Yes.'

'I liked doing that. But they didn't pick me for the lessons.'

'That doesn't matter – you liked it,' I replied. 'You should do some more. I remember – you were good at it.' I hadn't made that part up. Tio had been great at drumming. I could picture him so clearly tapping out a rhythm that seemed so complicated I couldn't understand how he was making it. Though I did believe what I was saying to Tio, I remembered the decision that I'd made to myself yesterday that I was never going to sing again. At just the thought of it, I felt my shoulders slump down, weighed down by the feeling that I really wasn't very good at it. Despite Tio telling me he'd been lying, his words had sparked a belief in me that I couldn't let go: that I'd made a fool of myself by trying. And it would be easier not to try any more.

'You really think I was good at drumming?'

I swallowed the negative thoughts about myself. 'Yes. And there's other things that you're good at too,' I said. 'You used to be a really good friend.'

'Used to be,' Tio muttered.

'Could still be,' I said back.

I found myself smiling a little and I looked over at him.

This time, his eyes met mine and he smiled back.

'You know, Layla hasn't had the easiest time. She acts like nothing can hurt her but she could do with another friend – other than me, I mean.'

'She hates me,' Tio said again.

'She doesn't know you. Not the real you, anyway. Just the one who's been acting like a . . . like an idiot.'

Tio started to laugh and as his face creased, I joined in. I couldn't help but think how much I'd missed this Tio, and how much we'd both missed out on in the last few months. 'I have been an idiot,' he agreed.

Tio looked into the distance and then his face crumpled. 'I can't stop thinking about how I've been treating you for the last few months. Aren't you still angry at me?'

'I'm . . . I was . . . upset. But no, I'm not angry with you,' I said. 'And I'm sorry if you think I've ignored you since Layla joined our school. I didn't mean to do that. But I can see it might have come across that way.'

'I wish ... I wish that I hadn't done those things,' Tio said sheepishly. 'I really am sorry.'

We were both quiet for a few moments. The wind streamed through the trees overhead. More leaves fell in dry, curled loops that skittered across the pavement noisily. I had an odd kind of feeling inside me – I was still worried and still felt lonely, but there was also a tiny surge of hope. I felt warmed by it, despite the cold wind that whipped around us.

'Can we be friends again, do you think?' Tio asked.

'Yes,' I said. 'But on one condition.'

'What?'

'You have to try to get to know Layla. I think you two will actually get on,' I said.

'Bit hard at the moment, isn't it?' Tio smiled again.

'Er, well, yes,' I said, laughing again. 'When everyone wakes up,' I added.

'You know this morning, when I saw you were awake too, I couldn't believe it. I kept thinking, no one else is awake, I'm all alone ... but if there could be one person who could be here with me, maybe it would be all right. And then I saw you. At that exact moment.'

'All right, you don't need to make stuff up.'

'I'm not,' Tio said. 'Honest.'

'Okay. I've already said I'll forgive you,' I said.

Tio held out his hand to me. 'Friends?'

I looked at his outstretched hand, at his eyes that were still so sad, like dark pools that I could have jumped into. I pulled him in for a hug. We used to hug a lot.

'Friends,' I whispered into his coat. I was struck by the scent of Tio. It was a mix of things: pencil shavings and chocolate, but it also made me think of looking up at the stars in the night sky. As I inhaled him, I felt an ache grow inside me. I'd missed him so much. I'd not let myself think that before.

I gave him one last squeeze then released him. When he glanced at me, his eyes looked a tiny bit twinkly.

CASE #41029973876628

Case Holder Notes:

WEDNESDAY

1.34 p.m.

Primary Subject and Companion Subject Energy
Tension and Connection Shift.

WEDNESDAY

1.37 p.m.

'So, what happened to you at Dodo's?' Tio asked me.

I told him about going to Dodo's flat and her not being there. I showed him the drawing I'd taken from Dodo's cardigan, then explained how all the others had been ripped from her notebook.

Tio studied the drawing. 'What's it meant to be?' he asked.

'I don't know,' I said. 'Dodo didn't know either. She thought it came from a dream. I mean, it might not have anything to do with all of this but . . .'

'You think it might,' Tio finished for me. He looked at the drawing once more. 'What did her note say again?'

I unfolded it from my pocket and handed it to him.

He read it out aloud, 'I've got to hide something. I'm being watched. I'm going to take it to the . . .'

Holding the note and the picture side by side, the black zigzag line on the note looked a bit like one of the scribbles on the creature she'd drawn.

I reached out for it and, as though Tio was reading my thoughts, he said, 'That zigzag – do you think she means this creature thing?'

'It could,' I said. 'I mean, it looks a bit like these marks here. But where is it? And how would we know where to find it?'

'You said she thought it came from her dreams ... so maybe her bedroom?' Tio asked.

'But there wasn't anything there,' I said.

'Hmm, well, if we can't work out what her note means, why don't we go to places she knows? Other than her flat, where else might she go?'

'Well, firstly there's her work. She has camera traps set up all over the place. I don't know exactly where they are, but she has an office, I think.'

'Have you ever been there?'

'No,' I said. 'Layla has, actually. Her mum has a space in the same building and they've seen each other there.'

'Let's try her office, then,' Tio said.

'I don't know where it is, though.'

'Why don't we go and see whether we can find the address at Layla's flat?' Tio asked.

'We'll have to try harder to get in this time.'

'Let's go,' Tio said, nodding. I thought he wouldn't remember the right way to Layla's, but he turned towards it as though he'd always known how to get there. We sprinted to Layla's flat, and after failing to find a front door key, we clambered over the gate into her garden.

We both pressed our faces to the window of Layla's bedroom. I spotted the pale underside of her arm again.

'Has she changed position at all?' Tio asked.

'She hasn't moved,' I said, unable to hide the disappointment in my voice.

'How should we get in?' Tio asked.

'I don't know. I don't want to smash the glass or anything like that . . .' I looked up at the tall windows.

'We should try the back door,' Tio said. 'Just in case.'

He bounded off towards the back door that I knew opened into Layla's kitchen.

'It's locked!' Tio shouted as he tried it. The door handle squeaked loudly in the quiet garden.

Suddenly, I heard a rustle from behind me. I spun round and noticed Tio was staring at the bushes like I had done.

'Did you hear that?' he asked.

'Yes,' I said.

'What was it?'

'A cat . . . or something?' I was suddenly very aware of how loud my heart was beating and how shallow my breaths were, but I told myself it was just a cat and I was only giving it any thought because I was already rattled.

'Sounds like a large cat . . .' Tio said.

We both stared at the bushes where we'd heard the rustle. I stared so hard that the greenery seemed to swim before my eyes, and the leaves no longer looked like leaves but like jewelled scales. There was no lashing tail of a cat or any other movement, but I couldn't peel my eyes from the leaves.

'I think it's gone now,' Tio said. 'Whatever it was.' He turned back to the door and kneeled down by the cat flap as he tried to open it.

I kept my eyes fixed on the bush.

I was about to turn away when I heard it.

Snap.

One of the branches in the bush was breaking and the whole thing shuddered.

'It's still there,' I said, my voice rising. My heart was beating a thousand times a minute. The same panicky feeling I'd had when I looked at Dodo's drawing of the weird creature coursed through my body – only this time, it was an even bigger, even bolder feeling of fear.

The way the bush had moved told me that whatever was hiding was large – large enough to be a person. My mind started to race. Though I'd longed to find someone else, I was scared to see what was in the bush.

'Who's there?' I asked. My voice sounded thin and afraid.

I sensed Tio beside me.

'Did you see something?' he said.

'No, but . . .'

I glanced towards the gate that we'd need to climb to get out of here. The garden was closed in by a high brick wall and overgrown bushes. The only way out was the way we'd come in.

'Is there anyone there?' Tio called this time.

The bush remained still. It was so still that I wondered if I'd imagined the way it had swung and shuddered before.

I wanted to turn away but something inside me stopped. Fear tingled through my shoulders and whispered against the bare skin of my neck.

'I think it's gone,' Tio said again but it sounded like he was trying to convince himself.

Then, the bush moved again. There was another crashing, breaking sound and its branches rustled so violently that it seemed like the bush had come alive.

I felt Tio's hand clutching mine. We backed away until we were pinned against Layla's bedroom doors.

131

I glanced at Layla's unmoving body through the crack in the curtains.

'Please wake up,' I heard myself whisper. I could imagine it so clearly. She'd fling open the door for us and we'd retreat into the safety of her flat, away from whatever, or whoever, was hiding out there.

I saw Tio look towards Layla as I spoke.

The next few moments passed in such a blur that I couldn't tell what happened first.

The bush shook violently again.

Tio squeezed my hand so tightly I thought he was going to crush it.

And then I heard another sound – but this time, it was from Layla's room.

Layla.

She had woken up.

CASE #41029973876628

Case Holder Notes:

WEDNESDAY – 1.57 p.m.

See: Error Report #41029973876628 #3: Primary
Subject + Companion Subject.
   See: Connection Report #41029973876628
#2: Primary Subject + Companion Subject = Girl #3.

WEDNESDAY

1.57 p.m.

Layla sat bolt upright in bed, and I thought I could hear her gasp through the window.

'Let us in!' Tio yelled, pummelling the glass.

'Layla!' I screamed.

She flew to the door as I had imagined she would, and flung it open.

Tio and I fell into her bedroom.

'Close the doors! Close the doors!' Tio shouted.

Layla didn't question us but swung the doors shut and pulled the bolt across to lock them.

She looked outside at the garden and I peered round her. But there was nothing to see. There was no one there. The emerald bushes were as still as statues.

Layla turned back to us. 'What's happening?' she asked, puzzled. She was dressed in an oversized stripy shirt, which looked like it might have belonged to someone else, and some baggy red pyjama bottoms. Some of her hair stood up in matted peaks.

'There's quite a lot to explain . . .' I started to say, but Tio cut to the point.

'Everyone's asleep today – apart from me and Ana,' he said in a burst. 'And you now.'

134

'Asleep?' Layla echoed.

'They won't wake up. Or *can't* wake up,' Tio added.

'Look,' I said, pointing to her funny little alarm clock. It doesn't have numbers, only dashes and Vs and Xs. 'It's the afternoon. You've been asleep all this time.'

'Everyone's been asleep all day – apart from you two?' She looked from me to Tio and I could see that she was trying to understand why the two of us were together, after everything that had happened. She was clearly struggling with this on top of the news that the whole world could not wake up.

'Try to wake your mum up,' Tio suggested. 'If you don't believe us. You won't be able to do it.'

Layla's face scrunched up as she tried to understand. Her expression was foggy from sleep.

'Hold on …' she said. She scuttled away and I heard her talking to her mum in the other room. Then she was back, looking a little paler than she had before.

'She's asleep. I couldn't wake her. Just like you said.' Layla sounded deflated.

I looked over at Tio, and we exchanged a silent look. We both knew what a shock it was to find out what was happening today. There was nothing to say. We had to give Layla time to digest the news.

'I'm trying to work out why you might be making this up or how you would have pulled this off, but I can't think of anything …' She looked lost in thought. 'So, everyone's asleep. I do believe you.' She spoke clearly but her eyes looked so wide and worried, I thought they might fill up with tears. 'I'm going to call my dad, just in case he's awake.'

Her mouth made a funny, twisting shape that also made me

135

think she might start crying, but her eyes remained dry and she told us steadily: 'I'll be right back.'

Tio looked over at me with wide eyes.

'She took that pretty well,' he said in an approving tone.

'I told you you'd like her if you gave her a chance.'

Layla came back a few moments later.

'No answer,' she said. 'I couldn't get through to Dad.' I could see her mind was racing with what she'd just learned. I wanted to reach out for her but she wasn't meeting my eye. Instead, she looked towards the glass doors leading to the garden.

'What was happening out there?' she asked suddenly. 'You both seemed afraid of something.'

'We don't know what it was, but there was something weird out there,' Tio replied.

'We thought it could be someone else who was awake but ... it was sort of hiding from us.' I thought back to the person Tio had seen this morning. 'Tio spotted someone else this morning, but they ran away and we couldn't catch up with them.'

Layla sat on her bed and then carefully folded her legs under her so she was sitting cross-legged. 'So, you two are the only ones awake right now, apart from maybe one other mystery person who's sort of hiding from you. And I woke up some-how ...' I could tell her mind was whirring and I was impressed by the way that she'd taken in everything we'd thrown at her. 'And you've got no idea how it was that I woke up?'

Tio shrugged and I shook my head.

'Hmm,' she said. 'If we could work that out, maybe we could wake other peopl—'

'Layla,' I said, interrupting her.

She looked at me properly then and I saw a mixture of

emotions flash behind her eyes. I felt a stab of sadness that we'd argued and I'd stormed away from her yesterday.

'I'm sorry about yesterday,' I said. 'I shouldn't have walked off at the end of the day like I did. I know you were just trying to help.'

'And I am too. I'm sorry as well, I mean,' Tio said.

Layla looked at me and then Tio. She was clearly trying to work out how things were between us.

'I suppose being the only people awake means that we've had to talk about the stuff that's happened between us,' I said.

Layla looked over at me. 'And you're okay?'

'Yes,' I nodded. 'We've talked it through. It was kind of silly...'

Tio cleared his throat a little and I gave him a look. 'It was just a misunderstanding but it's all okay now,' he added.

'That's good,' Layla said and glanced towards Tio.

'I really am sorry,' he said.

'What for?' Layla asked.

'I know I haven't been very friendly to you either.'

I thought Layla might say something like the reason for him not being friendly was all down to his insecurities, and I knew that would annoy Tio. But instead she just looked at him and said, 'It's all right.'

Tio looked back at her as if to say, 'Really?' and then back to me with his surprised, funny face – the one that appears when he can't believe his luck.

My heart swelled and I smiled at both of them. They smiled back.

'I can't believe you're awake,' I said in a burst. 'It's amazing! We came round earlier and tried to wake you through the window, but you didn't even stir.'

Tio joined in too: 'It's going to be all right, I think. We can wake other people up, I know we can.'

'Have you learned anything else about the sleeping thing?' Layla asked.

'No, not really,' I said.

'But there's Dodo,' Tio added.

Layla looked up at me quickly. 'What about Dodo? Is she okay?'

'I don't know,' I admitted. I filled her in on everything that had happened and handed her the note Dodo had left for me, along with the drawing of the creature that I'd taken from her flat.

Layla studied Dodo's sketch. 'It doesn't look like anything I've ever seen before ... but then something about the arms looks familiar. A bit like an octopus's limbs. And maybe its body shape is a bit like a large monkey.'

'We thought the zigzag line might be linked to the creature,' Tio said.

'Because of these spikes?' Layla's finger rested on one of Dodo's pointed scribbles.

'But we couldn't work out where that meant we needed to go,' I said.

'So we thought we'd try any place that was linked to Dodo, and Ana told us your mum worked in the same place,' Tio said.

'Brimmington House,' Layla confirmed.

'We were going to see if we could get into your flat so we could find out where it was,' I explained.

'Now I can do you one better,' Layla said. 'I'll take you there myself.'

WEDNESDAY

2.14 p.m.

I've been at Layla's mum's flat so many times before, but like everything today, it felt different. Without the sound of the little radio that's always on in the kitchen, the air felt thick and still. I realized I missed the smell of food being made and the sound of chatter and laughter in the kitchen, which is what it's like when Layla's mum is cooking.

'Why don't we try to wake up your mum?' Tio suddenly blurted out.

'We could try. But I just went in there and she was definitely not waking up,' Layla said.

'No, I mean all three of us, together. Somehow Ana and I woke you up – I think it was because we did it together. I don't know – maybe it's silly,' Tio muttered.

'No,' Layla said in that direct way she has. 'It's a good idea. Let's try it.'

The three of us walked into Layla's mum's bedroom.

'Mum,' Layla said. She ran towards her and shook her by her shoulders a little. 'Mum! You can wake up now.'

There was a slight tremor in Layla's voice, but I could tell she was trying to hide it. It reminded me how I'd done the same to my mum, how I'd cupped my hand to her cheek to feel her warmth. It felt like it had happened far in the past; not a few hours ago that morning.

'What was it you did to wake me up?' Layla asked, jolting me from my thoughts. 'Let's try to replicate it exactly.'

'I don't know,' I admitted. 'I mean, we were looking at you through the window so we weren't very close to you.'

'Okay,' Layla said. She took a few steps back. 'You would have been about this far away.'

We stood there watching Layla's mum continue to slumber. She didn't move.

'Did you say something?' Layla asked.

'I-I might have,' I said. 'Something like, *wake up* ... I can't remember exactly.'

'Do it again now,' Layla said.

'Okay ... wake up, wake up,' I said repeatedly. It was only a whisper at first, but it grew louder and louder each time I said it.

A long minute passed. Layla's mum didn't move.

'Wake up, wake up,' Layla started to say and then the three of us were saying it as though it were a chant.

I wasn't sure who stopped first but we fell silent, our eyes still glued to Layla's sleeping mum. I looked towards Layla who seemed like she was fighting away tears again.

'Well, I guess it was worth a try,' Layla said in a wobbly voice. She stroked her mum's hair a few times and I saw a tear glistening on her cheek.

'It's going to be okay,' I said as I leaned in to hug her. Tio looked like he was almost as upset as Layla. Maybe he was thinking about when he tried to wake up his family, too.

'I know, I know,' Layla said. She wiped away her tears. 'We've just got to keep thinking and trying. Is there anything else that you can remember about how you woke me up?'

Tio looked like he was about to say something but then he stopped himself.

'What is it?' I asked him.

'Only that ... we were holding hands,' he said. 'We'd heard that noise and didn't know what it was. We were backing away towards the door. Remember?'

'Yes, that's right, we were.'

'Let's try it,' Layla said, her voice still shaky. She was standing between us and grabbed both Tio's and my hands in hers. Her palm felt cold, but her grasp was strong and sure in mine. 'Say it again, Ana,' she said.

'Wake up, wake up,' I said once more.

Layla ran towards her mother's still body.

'Anything?' Tio asked.

'No,' Layla said. 'She's still asleep.'

We'd watched Layla's mum for a little longer before trailing back to the kitchen. We'd decided that we'd better eat something. Layla said we needed brain food before we headed off to Brimmington House, and as soon as she suggested it, I realized how hungry I was.

'Have you got any bread?' asked Tio.

'No,' Layla said.

'What about eggs, flour and milk?' he questioned.

Layla opened the fridge and started pulling things out and opening cupboards.

'What are you making?' she asked.

'Pancakes,' he said, pulling a frying pan off some hooks above the stove. 'That okay?'

'Oh, yes, please,' replied Layla.

Though I felt sure that it wouldn't connect, I called Dodo a few times from Layla's mum's phone. I got her voicemail again. Though I wasn't really expecting her to answer the phone, as I heard her recorded message start, a well of disappointment opened inside me. When the beep came, I hung up, unsure how to tell the others what was on my mind.

When I went back into the kitchen, Tio was standing at the stove, flipping a pancake onto a pile of others. The rich smell of melting butter filled the flat and I was transported back to yesterday morning, when Mum had cooked pancakes to cheer me up. Again, I was struck by how long ago that seemed – any time before today seemed distant.

Layla glanced over at me as I came back in. She had a smudge of chocolate just above her upper lip. Next to the pancakes there was a jar of chocolate spread with a knife sticking out of it.

'Are you okay?' she asked gently. Tio looked over too, his face full of concern.

I could feel the warmth from them both. 'Yes . . . and no,' I said. 'I just miss my mum. She made pancakes for me yesterday and I was remembering that – and her. And it's just . . .'

'We're going to wake everyone up,' Tio said with a sureness that I'd not heard from him before. 'We can do it. We'll work it out.'

'You woke me up, didn't you?' Layla pointed out. 'Tio's right – the three of us can do this.'

I looked from one to the other, and either because they spoke with such certainty, or because they seemed so united, I let myself believe them. I gave a little nod.

'First – eat,' Tio said and pushed the plate of pancakes in my direction.

I realized how hungry I was and took a round golden pancake, brushed it thickly with chocolate spread, rolling it up before cramming it into my mouth. Before I'd finished swallowing I was already making up another. A rush of sweetness filled my stomach and I had to remind myself to chew before swallowing.

Tio laughed at me, watching me scoff the pancake.

'Hungry, huh?'

'These are really good. As good as my mum's,' I said. 'Thank you.'

Tio gave me a tiny smile before ladling another dollop of mixture into the frying pan.

I can't remember how many we ate. We ran out of batter so Tio made even more. Only when we'd used the last egg did he stop cooking.

I was biting into my last pancake – I'd put so much chocolate spread in it that it was oozing out of the end, about to fall onto the plate – and I felt so full and contented that I didn't want to move. I wanted to stay right there in Layla's flat, eating pancakes away from the rest of the world.

As though she'd heard my thoughts, Layla said, 'We'd better get going soon. It'll get dark in a few hours.'

Tio gave a little groan and I wondered if, like me, he felt the same. Exhausted by today and wishing that he could hide away from it all.

'Are you both okay?' Layla asked.

'Yes, it's just it'll be hard to leave here. It's the first place today that's felt kind of normal,' Tio said.

'That's it exactly,' I said in a rush. 'That's just how I feel. I know we have to get going and I do want to find out what's happened, but another part of me just wants to stay right here and not have to deal with everything out there.'

I looked through the living-room window out into the garden. Nothing had changed. The bush that had been shaking was now still.

But then, as quickly as a shooting star bursts across the night sky, I saw a shadow dart across the garden.

My stomach flipped over in fear.

Someone, or something, was still outside.

WEDNESDAY

2.53 p.m.

My mouth was so full of pancake that the sound that I made was less 'Over there!' and more of a garbled choke.

'What is it?' Layla asked, springing up from her chair.

I pointed at the window. Tio spun round but the shadow was gone.

I swallowed and managed to speak. 'I thought I saw something out there.'

'What did you see?' Tio asked.

'It was a shadow of something or someone moving really quickly across the garden.'

Tio marched over to the window and peered out in every direction.

'I can't see anything now,' he said.

Layla looked too. Then she went to the back door that led to the garden.

'Don't open it,' I said instinctively.

Layla looked at Tio and then back to me again.

'We can't stay in here for ever – not if we want to try to find Dodo and work out what all this means,' Tio said gently.

'I know,' I said. 'But ... I definitely saw something. And, Tio, there was something in the bush, wasn't there?'

'Yes,' he said. 'But maybe it wasn't anything to be frightened of; it just looked that way. It could have been a couple of cats or squirrels even.'

I didn't answer back that there was no way it could have been either of those things. I couldn't explain it, but I knew it was something else. I had the same feeling of being watched that I'd had when I left Dodo's. I knew there was no real reason why I felt like that, but that didn't make it seem any less nerve-wracking.

'Come on,' Layla said. 'Have a look yourself.'

I took a few cautious steps towards the window.

'We'll be careful,' Layla said.

'And we'll stay together,' Tio added.

My hand had crept into my pocket and I was clutching Dodo's note tightly. We still had no idea what it meant, but I knew we wouldn't find the answers by staying put.

I swallowed my fear and my wish to stay safe in Layla's flat and looked outside into the shadowy garden. I knew I had to put my feelings to one side. We needed to go back out there and face whatever it was.

WEDNESDAY

3.12 p.m.

I'd been to Layla's dad's bike shop a few times, but never when it was closed. Layla said it would take us a while to walk to Brimmington House where Dodo worked so she suggested we borrow bikes from the shop. I tried to not look towards our building, which was down the road from here. More than anything, I wanted to go back and check on my mum but it felt urgent that we keep looking for clues to try to work out how we could wake everyone up. I pushed the thought of Mum from my mind, even though I desperately wanted to see her.

Layla took us round the back of the shop and unlocked the grey door with her keys.

'These ones are fast,' she said, leading us through the shop to point to a stand of bicycles that were decorated with fluorescent shapes.

We dithered for a moment, because we knew what we were doing was technically stealing even though it was Layla's dad's shop.

'It's okay,' Layla said, somehow reading my mind. 'My dad would understand why we need them. We'll return them anyway.' She chose the one that was closest to the door and started to wheel

147

it through the shop to the back entrance. Tio followed her lead and took the next one in the row, leaving me with one adorned with angular-looking dragons, their wings spread wide in flight.

I hadn't ridden for a while, but after a few wobbles my bike was slicing through the sharp, cold air.

Layla rode sure and fast across the road and Tio raced to catch up to her.

Though I knew I was only riding a bike, as the city streamed past us I had the feeling of flying, gliding through the air with the speed and grace of the dragons painted on my bike. With Layla to one side of me and Tio to the other, I felt far stronger than I had all day. We raced down the roads, and as we cycled towards Dodo's workplace, I felt a little bit of hope reignite inside me: maybe we would be able to find her.

Brimmington House was a dark, imposing building.

Layla dug around in her rucksack for the keys she'd taken from her mum, then slid one of them into the lock.

Part of me was worried that it wouldn't work but then the lock clicked open and Layla barged her shoulder against the door to open it up.

'Look,' Tio said, pointing towards a security guard. He was sitting upright on his chair, but as we approached, I could see that his head was leaning forward and he was clearly fast asleep. His tight curly hair was peppered with white.

'Oh, I see. There's everyone who was asleep in their beds because it was night-time, and then there's people who were awake because they were at work. This security guard looks like he fell asleep right in the middle of whatever he was doing,' Layla deduced.

I thought of Mum working the night shift at the hospital. 'Let's just hope whoever was working wasn't doing anything very important,' I said.

Our footsteps scuffed against the floor as we walked down one of the corridors off the reception, Layla leading the way. Automatic lights flickered on as we continued walking. It felt almost too bright after the dim bike ride over.

'Do you know where Dodo's office is?' I asked Layla.

She nodded. 'It's on the same floor as my mum's,' she said.

She stopped at the lift and pushed a button to call it.

A mechanical whirring noise filled the air as the lift travelled to meet us. Then there was a dinging sound as the doors opened. A monotonous voice intoned, 'Ground Floor.'

We climbed in together, pressed the button for our floor, and the lift jolted upwards.

We got off at the fifth floor where Layla led us through a set of double doors and down another corridor.

'Mum said that this used to be a paper-bag factory,' she said. 'This is the newer bit, but Mum's and Dodo's offices are in the older part of the building.'

We passed lots of colourful doors that had little rectangular signs that told us what was inside. I followed Layla as we weaved through more corridors and I knew how difficult it would have been to find Dodo's office if Layla wasn't here to help us.

We reached a part of the building that felt different to where we had passed through already. The temperature was colder, and it seemed like it hadn't been updated in a while. The lights didn't flicker on automatically as we walked, but Layla found a switch for the stairwell.

'Almost there,' she announced.

We passed two more doors before Layla started grappling with her mum's heavy bunch of keys.

'I think it's this one,' she said, pointing to the third door, but it took a few tries before she found the key that worked.

The door creaked open and Tio looked around for a light switch. Eventually, I heard a click as he flicked the switch and light flooded through the office cubicles.

'I know this place,' I said straight away, taking in the white walls and trailing houseplants. The harsh light and the pointed leaves told me that this was the place Dodo had called from last night.

'I thought you hadn't been here before,' Layla said.

'I haven't ... but this was where Dodo was when she called us last night. So ...'

'She might still be here,' Tio said, filling in the blank.

'My mum sits over there,' Layla said, pointing to an overloaded desk. 'And Dodo's desk is on the other side of that partition.'

Layla and Tio fell behind me as I walked over to Dodo's desk.

I could see the spiky leaves that I'd seen on Dodo's videocall, but I would have easily known it was her workspace anyway. The family of foxes I'd seen in her notebook stared out at me from photographs, and there were a couple of pencil sketches pinned up, just like the ones I'd seen in Dodo's notebook. There was a map of the area tacked on the largest portion of the wall. It had little stickers dotted all over it.

Dodo's laptop was open on her desk. Its screen was black but the little green camera light was blinking away.

There was no sign of Dodo.

WEDNESDAY

3.44 p.m.

'She's not here,' I said, even though that was immediately obvious.

'Let's look for clues,' Layla suggested. 'Can I see that zigzag line she drew?'

Layla started looking through some notebooks on Dodo's desk with the note laid out next to them. I knew she was looking for the zigzag line, but I could also see that Dodo's notebooks only contained her lopsided handwriting.

Tio tapped on the laptop keyboard and the screen sprang to life.

A videocall application had not been shut down. It was definitely the one Dodo used to call us last night. Tio pointed to my mum's number and the timestamp and we exchanged a look.

'We're getting closer,' he said.

I took a deep breath and tried to let it go softly, but it came out sounding like a heavy sigh.

'Are you okay?' Tio said in a concerned voice.

'I don't know,' I said. 'I just thought there might be something else here.'

'If this was where Dodo was when she called you, we're

getting closer,' Layla said. 'We just need to know what we're looking for.'

Layla's finger traced the words on Dodo's note and she read them to herself in a whisper: *I've got to hide something. I'm being watched. I'm going to take it to the . . .* When she got to the zigzag line, she fell silent.

'You're the one who's got to work this out,' she said. 'This is something only you can understand. Try to remember everything you and Dodo talk about – it's probably something that you spoke about recently.'

I nodded, but I was worried I might not understand what Dodo's note meant.

I tried to push that thought away and look at everything in Dodo's room with fresh eyes. The pictures of the foxes, the map that she'd pinned up – the answer to the note might be right in front of me. Layla kept going through the notebooks and Tio searched through her computer.

'It looks like she'd downloaded something,' Tio said. 'That's all I can find.'

'What was it?' I asked.

'I'm not sure – but the file name is Polden_Es_110321.'

'That's the Polden Estate.' I recognized the name immediately.

'The place they're going to tear down,' Layla added.

'It's been deserted for a long time but they haven't knocked it down yet. Dodo set up a camera trap there to spot the local wildlife,' I said, remembering what she'd told me. 'It's all boarded up, but she was sure that she would find something worth protecting there.'

'This file is probably a download from one of her camera traps,' Tio concluded.

'Look,' Layla said, pointing to Dodo's map. 'There's a sticker here on Polden Road – that's probably the estate. These stickers must show where she's put camera traps.'

'Yes, of course,' I said, feeling a bit silly for not working that out myself. I reached out to press the edge of a yellow dot that had started to peel away. It was next to the railway line so it must have been the one that she'd set up for the family of foxes.

'We should go there – to the Polden Estate,' Tio said. 'It's where Dodo is leading us. She said in her note that she was hiding something – perhaps it was something she saw from this file she downloaded. Maybe if we go to the estate, we'll see whatever she was trying to hide.'

Layla nodded in agreement and just as before, I was hit with another burst of hope that perhaps we were on the right track after all.

Layla had sat down in the office and drawn a map of how to get to the Polden Estate, so she led the way. She stopped from time to time to check we were going in the right direction.

After she turned down one road and then another, Tio looked over at me and shouted out, 'We're here again!'

We slowed our bikes to a stop so we could speak and shouted for Layla to come back.

'What is it?' she asked.

'This is where we were this morning,' Tio explained.

'When Tio saw the person who ran away from us,' I added.

'Are you sure?'

'I'm pretty sure,' Tio said.

'Well, let's keep our eyes peeled,' Layla said. We continued on our bikes, but slowed down a little bit.

As we turned down Polden Road, we could see the edges of the boarded-up estate.

We stopped at what looked like the entrance to the estate, but there was no way in.

'There must be somewhere we can climb over to get in,' I said. 'Dodo must have done it. Let's walk around the fence and see if we can find it.' I was trying to sound calm, but there was something uncoiling inside me, almost like the sensation right before you're about to be sick, a kind of unravelling and a dizziness that feels like it's rocking you from side to side. I didn't know whether it was coming from looking for Dodo, my deep worry about what had happened today or the feeling I hadn't been able to shake off since leaving Dodo's flat, that there was someone watching us.

'Okay,' Tio said. I glanced over at him and realized that he looked quite grey too. His skin and his eyes both seemed duller than normal.

'Are you all right?' Layla asked.

I wanted to explain how I was feeling, but I was worried if I opened my mouth to say something, I might throw up. The feeling had come on so quickly it was hard to tell if I was worried about what we were about to do, or if it was just the uneasiness of being here in the first place.

'I feel a bit funny,' I managed to say. I looked at Layla. Her eyes seemed kind of buggy and she was trying to take deep, controlled breaths.

'Me too,' Tio and Layla echoed at the same time.

'I hope it wasn't the pancakes,' Tio said. He tried to smile to make it into a joke, but his expression didn't reach his eyes.

We started to walk around the edge of the estate, trying

to spot a place where we might be able to climb over, but as we walked further, the uneasy feeling I had grew and grew. I remembered having the exact same feeling when Tio and I were here this morning before we got back to the main road after we'd chased the suspicious person Tio had seen. But it was more of an irritation then, a feeling of being unsettled. Now I found I could barely walk forward. I had to force my feet with every step.

I couldn't help but think of magnets. The way that if you try to stick two of the same side together, they repel each other and you can feel them pushing apart. Like there's an invisible barrier between them. It was almost like my whole body was repelled by this place. I took another step forward, then found I couldn't go any further.

Tio and Layla had stopped too.

Tio wiped his forehead, and I could see his face was clammy from the effort of moving. I looked over at Layla – she was also drained of colour.

'What's happening?' Layla asked.

I looked behind us. We'd only walked a little way from where we'd left our bikes. It felt like we'd been trying to walk forward for a while but we'd only covered about ten metres.

'What's wrong with us?' I asked, although I didn't expect an answer.

'It feels like walking through sticky treacle,' Layla said. 'And also like I've eaten nothing but treacle for a week – my stomach feels really weird.'

Tio swiped in the air in front of him, even though there was nothing there.

'What is it?' I asked.

'I just wondered if there was something invisible stopping us from being able to walk forward,' he said, and then added a little sheepishly, 'but that sounds silly.'

'It's not a silly idea,' Layla said. 'Maybe it's something like a spiderweb – but much bigger and completely invisible ...'

'But there's nothing there,' Tio said looking into the empty air. Layla trailed her hand in front of us anyway, feeling for the undetectable webs.

'I can't feel anything,' she said slowly.

'There's something stopping us from walking forward. There's got to be,' I said. My mind searched for an explanation although, like Tio, they all seemed silly and implausible. But I felt sure there was something actively stopping us. For starters, it was affecting us all, and it was too much of a coincidence that we were all feeling the same sickness I'd felt this morning. However, this feeling was much stronger than before, as though it had been magnified.

I turned so I was facing Layla and Tio. They both looked quite ill.

'Should we turn back?' Layla asked.

'I guess so,' I said, and a rush of disappointment mixed with worry flooded through me. We'd not been able to find Dodo's camera trap on the estate and we were no closer to finding Dodo herself. Our hunt for clues had come to another dead end.

CASE #41029973876628

Case Holder Notes:

WEDNESDAY – 4.05 p.m.

Proximity Alert #41029973876628 #3.
   Activate Defensive Shield: Level Seven.

WEDNESDAY

4.12 p.m.

'Why don't we try ...' Tio looked almost too worried to speak. 'Why don't we try holding hands? Like when we woke Lay—'

Before he had a chance to explain himself more, Layla and I both slipped a hand into his. Tio clasped my hand firmly, and I immediately felt a little stronger.

'Do you feel that?' Layla asked.

'Yes.' Tio nodded.

We all took a step forward together. The lurching nausea didn't feel quite as powerful as it had just moments before. We tentatively took three more steps.

'Everyone okay?' Layla asked.

'I feel a lot better than I did,' I said, and I meant it. I felt a little surge of strength run through me as Layla squeezed my hand. 'How is this working?'

'Who cares, as long as we feel better,' said Tio. 'Let's keep going.' When I looked over at him, his eyes were brighter and more twinkly.

We took another few steps forward, and with each one I felt stronger until the sick feeling had disappeared completely.

'Keep looking for a place where we can get over the wall,' I said. Only moments before it had felt impossible that we could walk even a little bit further, but now we were working together to find a way forward, getting one step closer to Dodo with every move we made.

I could only enjoy that feeling for a second, though, because in the next moment, as I scanned the wall for a way to get through, something impossible slid into view.

It was like nothing I'd seen before – it wasn't human, nor did it belong to any animal.

It was a long, thin arm. And it was sliding over the wall right towards us.

The rest of it came into view. It was the creature from Dodo's sketches. Its main body almost looked like a dome, and it had arms that were far too long in proportion.

It slunk down the wall with the grace of an orangutan, but I couldn't see anything like a face. It was covered in a kind of thick fur that stuck up in spikes, which looked like it might be scales rather than hair. It was a blackish purple colour, similar to shadows and night-time and emptiness. I thought back to the stub of black oil pastel on Dodo's bedside table and the scribbles she'd used it for.

'What, what . . . ?' I heard Tio stutter.

Though I couldn't see the creature's face, as in Dodo's drawings, I felt like it was looking right at us. Almost as if it was talking to us – but I couldn't hear any sound.

I was frozen in place. A mixture of terror and worry flashed through me, but at the same time I felt overwhelming confidence that this thing was not going to hurt us. It was something about the way it was moving: it seemed curious and a little nervous about us, rather than ready to attack.

It rolled a little bit closer to us. I thought it was scanning me, Tio and Layla.

Tio was rooted to the ground like me, but Layla took a tiny step towards the creature. As she did, it seemed to retract in on itself.

'It's okay,' Layla said in the soft, lullaby tone that she uses with every animal she meets. She slowly reached out a hand towards the creature and then stayed like that, absolutely still. The creature unfurled itself gradually and seemed to be looking at Layla's hand.

She then started to wave her hand from side to side, still incredibly slowly. More of the creature's tentacles started to emerge, and it began to follow the movement of Layla's hands.

'Hello,' Layla said. 'This how we say hello.'

Layla looked up at me and Tio, her eyes shining bright. 'Can you believe this?' she seemed to be saying to us.

I felt incapable of speaking. Tio was also silent and stood dumbfounded beside me.

'You're what Dodo saw,' Layla said very gently. It moved a little more towards the sound of her voice. It reminded me of the way that she could lure the grumpy cat in the school car park to her, even though it ignored everyone else.

'You're very unusual, aren't you?' Layla kept speaking in the same steady tone. 'Do you have a name?'

The creature seemed to tilt its head to one side, but didn't make any kind of sound.

'Maybe we could give you a name?' Layla was quiet for a moment and then she said decisively, 'Rollo. Hi, Rollo, I'm Layla. And this is Ana and Tio. Say hello,' she prompted us.

'Hello,' Tio and I whispered.

'I wish Rollo could tell us what's been happening today. I've got a feeling that it's got everything to do with you.'

I noticed then that it seemed to be staring directly at Layla. It had drawn its body up and extended two of its thin tentacles so it looked almost like us – walking on two legs. From the way it stood, it looked gentle yet somehow curious. It reminded me uncannily of Layla.

'Can you see what it's doing?' I asked the others. I let my gaze drift over the creature.

'It's copying us,' Tio said quickly. 'It's copying you,' he said to Layla.

Layla's face burst into a sunbeam and she laughed. For a moment I wondered if the sound would make the creature retreat again, but it seemed to have become more confident. It even mimicked Layla's laughter, the scales where its shoulders would have been shaking with it.

'How's it doing that?' Tio pondered and I knew what he meant. Somehow just by rearranging its scales and tentacles it made us think of Layla, even though it was just a blob with arms.

'It's doing you now!' Layla said to Tio, still grinning. I looked up and saw that Layla was right. Rollo was scuffing the ground ever so slightly with its feet, not quite picking them up high enough, exactly how Tio walks.

'Yes, it's dragging its feet a bit, just like you do,' I said.

'Oh, yeah, that *is* how I walk!' Then Tio started to do a silly dance and Rollo copied him again.

'Now you!' Tio said to me. 'It's changed now; it's copying you.'

I could see Rollo was trying to move like me. It almost looked like it had managed to make itself bigger somehow too – its fur-scales were puffed up, and its back was hunched over a little bit.

Rollo's 'shoulders' drooped down by its sides. Although it made itself look physically bigger, it was as though Rollo was also trying to make itself seem as small as possible at the same time.

Its steps padded loudly against the tarmac as it walked clumsily in a circle. I could see that if it straightened its back then its legs would be able to extend, and it wouldn't trip itself up. If it stood tall and let its shoulders spread out then it would be able to stride. It would be just fine.

I unconsciously unfolded myself as I thought these things. I let myself do what I thought Rollo should do and in response, it changed and walked with a straight back, standing tall. Its long legs extended effortlessly.

'That's better,' I said and I felt something drain away from within me. A kind of stiffness I hadn't realized was there had untangled itself from my spine.

I don't know why the next thing happened. Or if it was my fault, because of the way I spoke, but suddenly, Rollo's fur-scales all stuck out on end for a tiny fraction of a second.

It was like a porcupine sharply raising its quills.

Then they all dropped down and one of its tentacles swung out and curled around the nearest streetlight. After a few seconds, Rollo had used the streetlight to swing down the road, disappearing into the distance.

We were left there, open-mouthed, wondering if we'd imagined what we'd just seen.

CASE #41029973876628

Case Holder Notes:

WEDNESDAY – 4.12 p.m.

Primary Subject, Companion Subject and Girl #3 join hands.

Connection Energy between Primary Subject, Companion Subject and Girl #3 stronger than Defensive Shield.

Breach of Regulation 1.1928 to investigate at closer range.

Personal Note by Case Holder: Through breach of Regulation 1.1928, unusual unifying behaviour observed.

See alongside Connection Report #41029973876628 #1: Primary Subject = Companion Subject and Connection Report #41029973876628 #2: Primary Subject + Companion Subject = Girl #3.

Case Holder proposes continuation of Case despite regulation breaches.

CASE #41029973876628

SUPERVISOR NOTES:

BREACH OF REGULATION 1.1928.
    CASE CONTINUATION DENIED.
    PROCEED TO ABSTRACTION AND SUBJECT
WIPE.
    DISCIPLINARY ACTION OF CASE HOLDER
PENDING.

WEDNESDAY

4.27 p.m.

'What was that?' asked Tio.

'The creature from Dodo's drawings!' Layla said, her voice full of glee.

'I know, but what was it?' Tio asked again.

'It has to be an alien!' Layla exclaimed with absolute certainty.

'It can't have been. Aliens don't really exist!' said Tio.

Layla's and Tio's words swarmed around me, so close to my own thoughts that they seemed like an echo.

'What else could it have been?' I heard myself ask aloud.

'It was a ... It was a ...' Tio was stuttering and repeating himself, over and over. He looked quite green. 'It was some kind of creature,' he was saying now. 'It must have got out of the zoo. Or it escaped from a lab ...'

'Tio, there's not a creature like that anywhere on Earth,' Layla said.

'You don't know that – it might be something that you haven't seen before.'

'Have *you* seen anything like it before?' I asked.

'No, but, but ... there's loads I haven't seen yet. They're

always saying on those nature programmes Ms Randall plays that there's way more we haven't discovered in the oceans yet—'

'Yes, I know,' I cut in. 'Dodo always says we know more about the surface of the Moon than what's at the bottom of the ocean.'

'Exactly,' Tio said and then he frowned. 'And it just can't be an alien. Like a real alien, I mean, could it?'

'Well, we don't know for sure,' Layla said. 'Like you said, it might be something we haven't seen before but . . .' She left the sentence hanging.

'Whatever it is, it must have something to do with the reason why nobody's woken up today,' I said. 'And it links back to Dodo again. It was definitely the creature from her drawings.'

'It's all too . . . it's just too . . . unbelievable,' Tio finally replied, shaking his head.

I laughed. 'It's unbelievable that everyone won't wake up today! I think we know it's not just a normal Wednesday, don't we?'

'But why would it make everyone stay asleep?'

'Well, I guess, maybe . . .' Layla started to say.

'What?' Tio prodded.

'It's just an idea, but maybe because it wants to look around without everyone gawping at it,' Layla said. 'Imagine if aliens came and everyone saw them. They wouldn't be able to do anything. We'd send the police and the firefighters and the army in most likely. People would freak out.'

'That makes sense,' I said.

'I don't know,' Tio muttered.

'It's just a theory – like the ones we had earlier,' I said.

'There's another question that's worth thinking about,' Layla said. 'Why are *we* still awake? If it had a way of keeping everyone asleep, why did it let you two wake up? And how did *I* wake up?'

'Well,' I said slowly. 'There might be some error and we're not meant to be awake at all. For whatever reason, it didn't affect me and Tio last night. It could be a random glitch. Or ...'

'Or what?' Tio asked.

'It wants us to be awake,' I concluded.

I swallowed hard, but there was a lump caught in my throat that would not budge. I couldn't understand what this might mean.

WEDNESDAY

4.46 p.m.

We hadn't seen the creature again, but we decided to go in the direction it had disappeared to see if we could find it. It seemed like the best lead we had to locate Dodo.

We clambered back on our bikes and sped off down the road the way the creature had gone. We passed some overgrown bushes sticking out from someone's front garden and they reminded me of the ones at Layla's flat. I brought my bike to a halt with a squeal of the brakes, and signalled to the others to stop, too.

'I was just thinking, that creature must have been what we saw at your flat,' I said to Layla. 'It was hiding in the bushes.'

'I guess so,' Layla said.

'And you know the person you saw running away from us this morning – could that have been it then, too?' I asked Tio.

Tio shut his eyes as he tried to picture it. 'It was so fast, I didn't see it properly. Just the movement. Maybe it was. It just seemed to vanish. Maybe it climbed up something, like a building, the way it did one of these.' He gestured to the streetlight. 'I guess it could have been that thing after all. I didn't see it for long enough to know, if you know what I mean. Maybe it wasn't a person this morning ...'

'It was Rollo all along,' Layla finished for him.

'Why did you call it Rollo?' I asked Layla.

'Don't you think it kind of rolls when it moves?' Layla asked. 'I mean, it's not like anything else I've ever seen. It's a bit like a monkey and an octopus and a hedgehog, all rolled into one, but even that doesn't really describe it.'

'A hedgehog?' I asked. Nothing about the creature had reminded me of a hedgehog.

'The way it hid itself – you know, like how a hedgehog rolls itself into a ball.'

'So a mon ... octo ... hog, a *monoctohog*,' Tio said.

'A monoctohog.' Layla nodded in agreement. 'Rollo the monoctohog. It's got a ring to it, don't you think? I get the feeling that Rollo's friendly. But also a bit scared of us.'

'We're the ones that should be scared of him. Look what he's done to everyone!' Tio said.

'You're right, Rollo must be powerful to have been able to do all this. Also, how do you know Rollo's a he? It might be a she?' Layla replied.

'True. Maybe on the planet where Rollo's from they don't have males and females,' Tio suggested.

'Hold on,' I said. 'So you *do* think Rollo's an alien.'

'I don't know,' Tio said a little sheepishly. 'Maybe it's the only thing that makes sense today.'

Layla laughed out loud.

'What's so funny?' Tio said.

'Just what you said – you're right – seeing an alien today makes perfect sense. It's just ... I mean, today is off the charts,

169

isn't it?' Layla said. 'It's like that saying – stranger things have happened. But today it's just stranger things keep happening right now.'

'I never thought I'd be having this conversation,' Tio agreed.

'So we all think Rollo is an alien,' I said.

'Finally, something we can all agree on,' Tio said, a small smile creeping onto his face.

I looked from Tio to Layla and once again felt a rush of happiness that this was happening with both of them by my side.

WEDNESDAY

4.50 p.m.

The light was starting to dim quickly, and suddenly all I saw around me were shadows. Since we'd seen Rollo, I kept my eyes fixed on every corner, on every hiding spot, but I didn't see any signs of Rollo, no matter how hard I looked.

The absence of people felt bigger in the dark. There were no car lights, and no warm glow from windows. Nothing shone through the twilight.

I felt hungry for all those little scenes I noticed every day as I walked by. Each one was like its own little picture of people at home. There might be splodgy paintings pinned up to the window and a teddy bear looking out. Or people wrapped up on the sofa surrounded by the glow of a television. Or a room might not have anything in particular in it, but I could still see the warm light of a lamp. But now, every window was dark. They didn't look like homes any more, just empty spaces.

'Let's stop here,' Layla suggested after we'd been riding for a while. 'I think we should turn back. There's no sign of Rollo. Why don't we go back to the Polden Estate to see if we can find any other clues about where Dodo is?'

Tio and I nodded in agreement.

'Can I see Dodo's drawing again before we set off?' Layla asked. 'It's the only thing we have that proves Rollo's existence.'

I dug in my pocket for Dodo's drawing and unfurled it. We'd stopped under one of the streetlights and it illuminated the crumpled paper.

As quick as a whip, a shadow rolled in from around the streetlight.

'It's back,' Tio said quietly. His voice sounded small.

I looked over at Rollo, and seeing it for a second time gave me the chance to look at it a little more. The way its spines moved was incredible; I'd never seen a creature who was able to use them in that manner. Just as before when it mimicked each one of us, it seemed able to express so much by the way it moved them around. As it rolled slowly in our direction, I got the impression it was trying to be careful and not scare us. I can't explain how exactly I knew that, but something about the gentle way it was moving its spines told us not to worry or be scared.

As Rollo came closer, I realized it was coming towards me. Though I knew it wasn't being aggressive in any way, I couldn't stop myself from holding my breath in anticipation.

One of its arms reached out to me and I heard an intake of breath from Tio, but Rollo didn't touch me at all. It reached for the drawing I was holding and plucked it straight from my hand.

'Oi!' I said, despite my nerves. Layla kneeled slowly, edging closer to the creature. The way its spines reacted when I said 'Oi' made me think it knew it was being mischievous.

'That's you,' Layla said, pointing to the drawing. 'Ana's aunt did it. She's seen you too. I wonder when that was.' Layla scrunched her nose a little, the way she does when she's thinking hard.

'When did Dodo do this drawing?' she asked.

'She didn't know,' I said. 'I saw it for the first time yesterday evening. It definitely wasn't there when I looked at her sketchbook last week so it must have been between then and last night.'

Rollo seemed to peer at the picture again, then tucked it into its body, as if it had pockets, and its arm reappeared without the drawing.

'Hey, give that back,' I said in protest and reached out towards Rollo. But it moved away quickly.

'We need it,' I said pointlessly. I had the oddest thought again that Rollo seemed to understand what I was saying – that I wanted the drawing – but it was not going to give it back to me. I felt frustration claw through me, and despair too. That drawing was the only proof we had that Rollo was real, but it also felt like my last link to Dodo and where she might be.

'Give it back,' I pleaded.

But Rollo gripped the streetlight and slunk away out of view.

'It's gone again,' Tio said as we peered into the shadows.

Layla started making clicking noises to encourage Rollo to come back and Tio called out to it. I stared into the darkness in the direction it had disappeared as though I could will it to return and give me back Dodo's crumpled drawing.

But it didn't.

'What if … what if … what if that alien thing captures us or does something worse …?' Tio looked over at us with wide, worried eyes.

'I don't think it's going to do that,' I said. 'It's weird but just now when I watched it, it actually seemed kind of friendly. I'm more annoyed that it stole Dodo's drawing.'

'Well, I think we should still be wary of it,' Tio said. 'We don't know anything about it.'

The list of all the things we didn't know seemed overwhelming and endless. I thought about suggesting that we write it all down, but it would have been so long that I decided not to. We did need to keep trying, though, to find Dodo – and to find Rollo too, now, I realized.

'We've got to find it,' I said. 'Rollo's the key to all this.'

'But aren't we meant to be looking for Dodo?' Tio asked.

'We know Dodo saw Rollo because of the drawing. Finding her might lead us to it or the other way round. Let me check Dodo's note again,' Layla said.

I passed it over to her, and as she examined it, I remembered that we'd come no closer to understanding what the zigzag line meant.

'Is Rollo back?' Tio asked all of a sudden, pointing across the road.

There was a flash of movement between the parked cars ahead of us.

'It's just a fox,' Layla said, looking up from Dodo's note.

'*Vulpes vulpes*,' I murmured.

We watched the shabby-looking fox plod across the road. It did not look at all bothered by us being there.

The silence was interrupted by chimes from a church tower nearby.

'What time is it?' Layla asked.

'It's five o 'clock,' Tio said, glancing at his watch.

'Five o'clock, already?' Layla sounded disappointed.

I looked towards the clock on the church tower anyway. It had an old, ornate face with black numbers. They weren't made

174

up of normal numerals, but were the same as on Layla's alarm clock, with lines instead.

I looked away from the clock for just a second and realized what I'd been missing all along.

'The five on your clock!' I said. I couldn't get the words out fast enough.

'What clock?'

'The alarm clock by your bed,' I said, pointing towards the church tower. 'It's a "V"!'

'Yes,' Layla said. 'Why?'

'V. V. V.,' I said in a rush. 'I know what it means. I know where Dodo is!'

My words kept coming out tangled because I was in such a hurry to try to explain what I had realized.

'What do you mean, V. V. V.?' asked Layla.

'It's not a zigzag line – it's three Vs joined together,' I managed to spit out. 'And it means "Five *Vulpes vulpes*"! *Vulpes vulpes* is the Latin name for foxes and a V by itself means five. It says, "Five Foxes".'

'But what does that mean?' Tio said.

'There was a family of five foxes that Dodo was watching by the railway. She told Mum and me about them yesterday. That's where she means, I'm sure of it.'

'Let's go, then,' Tio said, throwing himself back on his bike.

'Do you know where to go?' Layla asked.

'Yes, I saw the coloured dot on her map – I think I know roughly where it is,' I said.

'Well, lead the way, then!' Layla exclaimed, jumping onto her bike.

I'd never cycled faster than that ride over to the railway. I could feel my legs burning, but I kept pushing harder and harder despite the pain. I felt energized by the hope that we might have discovered something. I could feel it in every part of my body, from the tips of my fingers that were clasped tightly on the bike's handlebars to the ends of my hair that splayed out behind me. After trying hard and getting nowhere for what felt like forever, we were finally moving forward.

As we rode, we passed by more foxes who were skulking in the shadows. Each time I saw one I pedalled faster. Seeing them also made me chide myself for not realizing earlier what Dodo's clue had meant. We'd spoken about the family of foxes just last night!

As we pulled up to the railway, I thought of Dodo's drawings – not the scribbled sketches of Rollo, but the family of foxes in the first half of her notebook.

Then Tio called out to me, and I saw Layla pointing ahead of us.

I felt myself balloon with upset.

Lying on the path in front of us was Dodo's crumpled, sleeping body.

WEDNESDAY

5.32 p.m.

I ran towards her. I could see her satchel slung over her body and her scarf bunched around her face. Tio shone his bike light towards her so I could see that her eyes were shut, her face crumpled in a heavy sleep.

'Dodo!' I called out. But even before her name left my mouth, something swooped in beside her.

It could have been a shadow but it was too dense.

It was darkness – the darkest, blackest black I'd ever seen.

Spines rippled across its back.

A monoctohog.

I could tell immediately that it wasn't Rollo. This one's spines seemed to be clashing together in anger.

And it was coming right for us.

CASE #41029973876628

SUPERVISOR NOTES:

ABSTRACTION AND SUBJECT WIPE
UNCOMPLETED.
   INTERVENTION REQUIRED.
   FORCIBLE ABSTRACTION AND SUBJECT
WIPE BY SUPERVISOR RECOMMENDED.
   FURTHER DISCIPLINARY ACTION OF CASE
HOLDER PENDING.

WEDNESDAY

5.36 p.m.

Layla and Tio almost crashed into me from behind.

'That's ...' Layla gasped as she spotted the monoctohog. 'That's not Rollo.'

This creature was much bigger than Rollo, but more than that there was a different energy in the air surrounding it. There was none of Rollo's curiosity. This monoctohog moved with an air of inflexibility. Though, like Rollo, it had no discernible face, I could somehow tell its expression from its stance.

It was one of pure anger.

A roaring filled my ears, even though the only sound I could hear was my own breathing, which was coming in ragged gasps. Fear slid through me. It seeped down my spine, pooling in my stomach.

The monoctohog seemed to have engulfed Dodo. I couldn't make out any part of her under its black body. Then one of its tentacles slowly reached out towards me.

I knew I needed to turn. I knew I needed to run, but the sight of the tentacle growing and reaching immobilized me. I couldn't move my feet. I told myself to run, but I couldn't take a single step.

I heard Tio scream, 'AAAAAAAANAA—!'

But the last part of my name was lost as Tio dashed towards the monoctohog. Its tentacle whipped him away as easily as one might bat aside a fly.

Tio flew through the air. When he landed there was a hollow sound, like something had broken.

Layla raced towards Tio and reached him before I did. His body had landed in such an odd way that it took me a moment to work out where his head was, what was his arm and what was his leg. I saw Layla linger over his body like me, trying to find his face. Then she kneeled and, taking care not to touch any of his limbs, laid a hand against his cheek.

'Please be okay,' I heard myself say. I was holding my breath.

Tio's eyes were sealed shut as though he too was lost in a sleep from which he could not be woken.

'Tio. Tio,' Layla was saying gently. He gave no sign of hearing her.

'You're going to be okay,' I heard her whisper.

Tio gave the tiniest cough. Even though it was just a cough, it was the most amazing sound I'd ever heard.

Tio's eyes flickered open and met Layla's.

'You're going to be okay,' she said again. 'Can you walk?'

'I don't think so,' Tio said. He looked like he was in pain.

'Where are you hurt?'

'I don't know,' he mumbled. 'Everywhere.'

My eyes met Layla's. *What are we going to do?* I thought.

I was awash with emotions. I felt the lashing spike of anger that this monoctohog had hurt Tio, but deep inside I felt very, very scared. Tio's worries about what the monoctohogs might do to us were very real now. Rollo had seemed friendly, but it was only one of them. How many more could there be? I imagined what it might look like if I had spines myself. They'd be standing up in fear, showing exactly how I was feeling.

I looked back at Dodo and the monoctohog, then at Tio, lying injured and still before me.

If only Dodo could wake up.

If only Tio could walk.

But we were stuck.

Then the monoctohog reared up, its body so large it seemed to block out the entire sky and I heard Layla scream.

WEDNESDAY

5.49 p.m.

A whooshing sound filled the air. Layla and I both turned to look. Something flew towards the giant, rearing monoctohog. It looked like a large black ball, but as it sliced through the air, it started to open up and we could see its tentacles protruding outwards.

'Rollo,' Layla whispered.

The whooshing was coming from him. With a heavy thump, he knocked into the other monoctohog and everything was suddenly silent.

Then the monoctohog was thrown off Dodo, and both it and Rollo rolled to one side of her.

I could see Dodo again and Layla and I ran over to her. We each hooked an arm under her body and started to drag her towards where Tio was still lying.

I glanced back towards Rollo. Its tentacles were hanging limply by its side, but from the corner of my eye, I glimpsed the other monoctohog starting to rise. I felt like I was wearing my fear outside my body, like it was a heavy coat I was dragging alongside me, on top of the weight of Dodo. But my fear was also sharp and needling, and as soon as I realized that the other monoctohog was rising, I could feel it become pointed like a blade.

'Quickly,' I breathed to Layla, but dragging Dodo's sleeping body was difficult.

The other monoctohog had already started to make its way towards us.

'It's coming,' I heard Layla say, panic in her voice.

We tried to move faster but it was hopeless – dragging Dodo slowed us down.

The monoctohog's tentacle unfurled itself towards us, reaching out to Layla. I knew that it would bat her away as it had done to Tio.

'Let go!' I shouted to Layla. 'You've got to let go of Dodo!'

Layla hesitated, but then she managed to let go and jump out of the way just before the tentacle would have slammed into her body.

I knew I would have to do the same. The tentacle swished around as if angry that it had missed Layla. It lashed out towards me with an unexpected swing and fear shot through me.

'ANA!' Both Layla and Tio screamed my name. In that moment, it sounded like they had a single voice.

My hand was still gripping Dodo's coat tightly. I could feel the woollen fabric as though it had become my second skin. I knew then that I couldn't let go of Dodo, even though there was nothing I could do to help her. My mind flashed up the memory of Tio being thrown to one side as though he were a floppy old teddy flung away by a toddler.

I closed my eyes, waiting for the impact.

WEDNESDAY

6.01 p.m.

Big moments are meant to slow us down. I'm sure I've read that somewhere. But I remember what happened next as a blur, a rush of feelings and an explosion of senses.

It was as though I could feel the tentacle lashing me away from Dodo before it had even happened. I imagined I was already flying away from her, already crashing to the ground.

And then what would happen to Dodo? The monoctohog that was not Rollo looked like it was going to take her away. But where and for what? I couldn't shake the terrible feeling that if it took her then we'd never see her again.

But we had nothing we could use to stop it. Tio was injured, we didn't have any weapons and even if we did, how we would use them against a creature with multiple arms that was able to move in ways we couldn't imagine?

Rollo still lay where it had landed, an unmoving hump on the ground. It had tried to help.

There was nothing left to do.

It was just me, clutching Dodo, refusing to let go of her.

There was only me.

I shut my eyes and imagined I wasn't there with Tio and Layla any more. I was back in Dodo's flat.

I'd jumped back to a memory from a Chewy Tuesday, a long time ago. The radio was playing, and Dodo suddenly turned the volume up high so the song filled the room. She sang along with it, jiggling and dancing and making me do a twirl.

'Sing with me, Ana,' she said.

I sang because she told me to. I sang because it was all I wanted to do. I sang because the music was in my body and it felt like all I had to do was open my mouth and let it out.

'Wow!' said Dodo, collapsing on the sofa when the song finished. 'Ana, you have a beautiful voice.'

'I don't know,' I said.

But Dodo shook her head. 'No, you have. That's not up for question.'

I sat down next to where she'd landed on the sofa, slightly out of breath from dancing and singing. 'Do you like singing?' she asked me.

I nodded.

'Then you should do it, you know.'

'I don't think I'm good enough ...'

I heard Dodo take a deep breath before she spoke.

'I used to feel like that, too. I thought I wasn't good enough to do the things I liked doing. I don't think I've ever told you this, but when I first decided I wanted to be a naturalist, Granny was so cross with me.'

'Why?'

'She had other ideas about what she wanted me to be and worried that I couldn't make a living as a naturalist. She wanted me to do something safer. She might have been concerned I wasn't good enough, too, I think. She didn't say it to be mean, she was just genuinely worried and wanted the best for me. The night before I left for university, I was so nervous, I wasn't sure whether it was the best thing ever or the worst mistake I'd ever made . . .' Dodo looked so lost in remembering that it seemed she wasn't going to say anything more.

'What? What happened?'

'I failed my exams.' And then Dodo clapped her hand against her thigh and threw her head back in laughter. 'I left the course. I thought I *had* done the wrong thing, that Granny was right.'

'What did you do?' I spluttered.

'Well, it was awful. I came back home and started working any job I could get. I wanted the ground to swallow me up. But someone did believe in me.'

'Who?' I asked.

'Your mum,' Dodo said. 'You were tiny at the time. I remember it so clearly: you were tottering around with handfuls of stones in your fists. You wouldn't let them go. No matter how much we tried to persuade you and distract you with other toys or make it into a game, you just kept hanging onto them. I'd got back from some cleaning job I was doing and your mum looked at me and said – you've got to be more like Ana. Hold on to what you want! We laughed and laughed. But I knew that she was right. So I reapplied and got on to another course. Then I volunteered and worked as hard as I could. And I did it.

'The reason I'm telling you all this, Ana, is because all you can do is try. And be brave. Know that you might fail but don't let that stop you. Just promise me something – don't ever let the thought that you're going to fail at something stop you, okay?'

'Did you ever fail again?'

Dodo chuckled. 'Of course. But I just kept on trying. That's the most important thing to do.'

'But I'm not like you,' I said. 'I'm not confident. I don't think I could sing in front of people.'

Dodo looked me straight in the eye. Her eyes were such a dark brown that I felt like I was plunging into two pools of molten chocolate. But I could see fire in them.

And so, even though the monoctohog was bearing down on me, I did the only thing that I could think of. The thing that always brought me joy. The thing that I loved to do most in the world. If this was going to be my last day on Earth, then this is what I wanted to be doing.

I took a deep breath, filled my lungs, and sang.

WEDNESDAY

6.03 p.m.

The first note pierced the quiet of the night. It made me realize again how silent the world was without the noise of everyone else around us. I sounded louder than I thought was possible.

I was back on the stage in the school hall, imagining I was filling it with my voice, only now the whole world was my hall. The night sky was my ceiling.

Tio was in front of me again, but this time he was smiling at me, nodding, talking to me with his eyes, which were saying, *keep going!*

The moment passed.

And still I sang.

And still the monoctohog had not knocked me away from Dodo.

I opened my eyes and saw that the monoctohog was frozen, its tentacle just a few centimetres from my chest, hanging in the air near where my heart was beating and my lungs were filling as I continued to sing.

I glanced towards Layla and Tio and saw that their faces looked almost identical – both of their mouths were wide open in astonishment.

I sang and I sang and I sang and my voice only faltered once, for just a second, when I knew I was coming towards the end of the song. I wasn't sure what I should do. I'd stopped the monoctohog by singing, so if I stopped singing, would it keep going?

Fear darted through me once more, but then I glimpsed a movement out of the corner of my eye and realized that Rollo was rolling slowly in my direction. One of its tentacles unfurled towards the other monoctohog's tentacle that was still pointing, frozen, at my chest, and gently led it away from me.

I reached the end of the song and tried to make the final note last as long as I could. I finished with a gasp. I took a deep breath and waited, hoping that against all odds I had done enough.

CASE #41029973876628

SUPERVISOR NOTES:

DUE TO THE EXTRAORDINARY BEHAVIOUR
BY PRIMARY SUBJECT OF 'SINGING',
CONTINUATION REQUEST OF CASE
#41029973876628 IS GRANTED.

FURTHER DISCIPLINARY ACTION PENDING
FOR CASE HOLDER FOR MULTIPLE BREACHES
OF REGULATION 1.1928.

SUGGEST RE-ALLOCATION OF CASE
HOLDER FOLLOWING TERMINATION OF CASE.

WEDNESDAY

6.10 p.m.

The monoctohogs were speaking to each other. At least that's what I thought they were doing. Their spines were moving, falling in and out in a rhythmic pattern, a little like a line of dominoes falling. The spines weaved up and down, over and over. It was hypnotic to watch. Their tentacles were still connected from when Rollo had reached out to the one that was pointed at me. Although I could hear no sound, I could tell they were communicating.

My grip was still tight around Dodo. My arms ached from holding her up, from grasping her so strongly, but at the same time they felt like they'd turned into something more than skin and bone. They were as hard as metal, as unmovable as stone. I wouldn't let her go.

Finally, the monoctohogs' spines relaxed and they both turned slightly towards me, or at least that's what I thought they were doing as I still couldn't make out their faces.

The larger one, the one that was not Rollo, seemed to be looking right at me. As though it were trying to commit me to memory. Then it rolled away slightly and one of its tentacles unfurled to grasp a streetlight, before it swung away.

As soon as it left, Layla, who was holding Tio up, hobbled towards me.

'You were amazing!' they said at the same time, as if they'd planned it. They turned towards each other and burst into laughter.

I felt happiness swell through me as I took in what they were saying: that I *could* sing, that I could do it. It was like I was full of bubbles.

'How did you know to do that?' Layla asked, breathless with laughter.

'I didn't,' I said. 'I didn't think. I knew there was nothing that I could do and so I might as well ...'

'Do the thing you love,' Tio finished for me.

'It was incredible,' Layla said.

Tio kept talking as Layla helped him to sit down. 'The monoctohog stopped like a second, no – a tenth of a second, no – a hundredth of a second before it was about to knock you down.'

Rollo had stayed close by and rolled itself a little nearer to where Dodo still lay in my arms, sleeping.

'I wish you could tell us what was going on,' Layla said, looking over at it.

'It's interested in Dodo – it must have something to do with the thing that she said she was hiding.'

'If only we could wake Dodo up,' Tio said.

'But we haven't worked out how you did it to me,' Layla said.

'I've been thinking about that,' I said. 'In that moment, we were, you know, pretty scared. We thought there was someone in the garden, remember? And we really, really needed you to wake up. I don't know about Tio, but I imagined you waking up. I pictured it happening. And then you woke up after I did that.'

'I did the same!' Tio exclaimed.

'Well, I think that could have been what did it. We were both thinking that in that moment, wanting it to happen so much that we could picture it clearly.'

'But didn't you do that when we tried to wake up my mum?' Layla asked.

'No, I know what Ana means,' Tio said. 'We did try before, but it wasn't crucial that she woke up. We weren't really trying as hard because it wasn't the most important thing in the world.'

'So, we must try really, really hard to think that Dodo will wake up. We've got to picture her doing it. Because we have to understand what's happening. The world can't be like this for ever. We have to really, really want it, need it, all together, at the same time ... then it might work,' I finished with a gasp. It felt a little exhausting to imagine using all our strength to try, or even to think about trying it. After the singing, it was almost too much, but a little spot of hope sparked in me.

'I mean, it might not work,' Tio mused.

'But it's definitely worth a try,' Layla said.

'Definitely,' Tio and I agreed.

'Shall we hold hands again?' Tio asked.

'Yes,' I said. 'Let's do that too.'

We linked hands and started to think. This time I didn't just ask for Dodo to wake up in a tiny whisper, I filled my mind with it. Suddenly, it was like I could see Layla and Tio's thoughts. It felt as though they were slipping through the air, a golden stream, connecting with each other, becoming stronger and stronger and stronger.

Then, all of a sudden, Dodo blinked. A blink so small I

thought I had imagined it. But then she blinked again and sat up, rubbing her eyes.

I heard Layla shout, a sound of wonder and happiness, and Tio stood beside me, clenching my hand fiercely. He didn't need to put it into words because I could feel it too. Relief ran through me – we were no longer the only ones awake and we could wake other people up. Everything was going to be all right.

CASE #41029973876628

Case Holder Notes:

WEDNESDAY – 6.19 p.m.

See: Connection Report #41029973876628 #3:
Primary Subject + Companion Subject + Girl #3 =
Primary Subject Relative.

WEDNESDAY

6.19 p.m.

'Ana?' Dodo sounded groggy, her voice coming out as a hoarse whisper.

'You're awake! You're awake!' I couldn't stop myself from chanting. I felt full of happy bubbles, just like before, only now I was double-packed with them. I felt as though I could blast off from the ground! I couldn't stop looking at Dodo, at the way she raised her hands to her eyes to rub them, how she looked around, how she yawned. Every single movement was a miracle.

Tio and Layla were grinning and whooping, identical delighted expressions on their faces. We'd done it. Our plan had actually worked.

I could see Dodo was trying to piece it all together – why we were all there by the railway at night.

'Layla? Tio? What's happening? Why are you here?'

She slipped her hand into her pocket and looked around.

'Do you want to tell her or should I?' Tio said, looking over to me and Layla.

'Well, you have a knack for it,' Layla said.

But before Tio could say any more, Dodo's voice rose sharply.

196

'Get behind me,' she said. Her eyes had lit up with fear. She reached out and huddled the three of us closer to her.

'What is it?' Layla asked. Then she spotted Rollo ahead of us and said, 'You don't need to worry about Rollo. It's friendly.'

'Rollo?' Dodo said.

'We've named it,' I explained. 'Listen, Dodo – a lot has happened today.'

'Today? What do you mean today? I saw you a few hours ago,' Dodo said, still looking over anxiously at Rollo.

'It's Wednesday evening. You've missed a whole day,' I said. 'This morning when I woke up, no one else was awake.'

'They're still not awake,' Tio added. 'Listen – can you hear any traffic, or any noise at all?'

'What?' Dodo rubbed her temples. 'No one's awake? How? Why?'

'We were hoping you might know the reason why. You left me this note and we worked out what you meant – five *Vulpes vulpes*, the five foxes. What are you hiding here?' I asked, passing her the note, which was now very crumpled and worn from handling.

'It was after you left this evening, I mean – yesterday evening. I couldn't sleep. I was pacing around my flat and I knew I wouldn't be able to get any rest. So, I decided to go to my office and look at some of the camera trap footage I have. I saw there was a file from one of my newer cameras that I thought I'd not used because it was back at home. But it's one that uploads straight to my computer. That's when I saw it, on the screen,' Dodo explained.

I noticed her hand was back in her pocket, feeling for something.

'What did you find?' Layla asked.

'It was . . . you,' Dodo said, still looking towards Rollo a little fearfully. 'It was when I was at the Polden Estate on Monday night, setting up the trap with the new camera. There was a film that showed me seeing it and then it grew these long tentacles. It touched me, then it suddenly disappeared. And then in the film, I just pack up the camera. I think I just go home.' Dodo looked stiff, remembering, her eyes dark with worry.

'Rollo must have been the reason why you lost your memory,' I said in a rush. 'It didn't want you to see it, it wasn't meant to be seen. But it didn't do a great job. You did all these drawings of it. You didn't remember exactly what had happened, but you hadn't forgotten meeting Rollo entirely. You thought it was from your dreams. And you forgot things that you'd usually know – like Chewy Tuesdays.'

'It does seem that's when I started forgetting things,' Dodo agreed.

'And you thought you were being followed too, didn't you?' I asked. 'Do you remember calling us last night and leaving the note?'

'Yes,' Dodo said, rubbing her forehead as if she were still trying to wake herself up. 'I couldn't really explain why I thought I was being followed, because I never actually saw anything, but I just had a sense I was being watched. But every time I looked for someone, there was no one there.'

I nodded. I knew that feeling very well. 'That must have been Rollo. You followed Dodo,' I said, turning to Rollo. 'You knew where she lived. Perhaps you realized you'd not done a very good job of wiping her memory, so you checked to see if she'd made any record of you. And you found something. You took the drawings she made of you, didn't you?' I spoke softly to Rollo, remembering how I'd thought Dodo's flat had been searched by her, or by someone else. I'd have never imagined Rollo the monoctohog doing it.

Slowly, Rollo reached its tentacles into more invisible pockets on its body and took out pages and pages of Dodo's sketches. Among them was the note Tio and I had written and left by the school gate.

'You do understand me!' I said.

Rollo was absolutely still.

'Am I right?' I asked Rollo. 'Did you wipe Dodo's memory?'

Rollo swept all its tentacles back into its hidden pockets in one swift movement. Then it pointed towards Dodo very, very gently and made a kind of circle in the air around her face.

'I think that's a yes,' Layla said.

'You tried to stay secret,' I said. 'That's why you removed all the things that have traces of you – Dodo's memory, the pictures, our note on the school gate ...'

'But what about us?' Tio asked. 'We've seen it.'

I looked straight at Rollo.

Even without a face, I could tell it was looking at me gently.

'I think it will wipe our memories too,' I said.

'But why do any of this?' Tio said. 'Why let us see it? Why make everyone sleep and keep only us awake?'

'I don't know.' A hundred thoughts were whizzing around my brain, trying to find an answer, but all I knew was that I was completely confused.

'Maybe,' Dodo said, crouching down and looking at Rollo attentively, 'it's like when I'm looking at wildlife. I don't want my presence to prevent animals from doing what they would normally do. That's why camera traps are so good – because I'm not there at all, but I can still watch them. But sometimes they do see me. Sometimes I might disturb them because I can't help but want to watch them in real life as I'm so interested in them.'

'So, Rollo's been watching us and trying to learn why we do the things that we do . . .' Tio said.

'Like a kind of experiment?' Layla asked.

'Maybe,' Dodo said.

'And he got too close and wanted to see us,' I finished.

Dodo shrugged.

'You should have seen what happened, Dodo. What Ana did.' Layla said. 'There was another one – another monoctoh—'

'A what?' Dodo interrupted.

'Monoctohog,' Tio explained. 'That's what we've called them.'

'Because they're a bit like a monkey, an octopus and a hedge-hog combined,' Layla said.

'That makes sense,' Dodo said with a small smile.

'The other one – it looked like it was going to take you or something,' Layla continued, 'but Ana wouldn't let you go. And then it was going to swipe her away just like it did to Tio. He flew through the air and landed really badly.'

'Are you okay?' Dodo asked him, looking alarmed.

'I'll be all right,' Tio said, although I realized that he was still standing awkwardly, clearly in pain from his fall. Rollo rolled over and brushed up against him gently, just as a cat might do. Tio made a funny kind of sound, a little like a sigh and a laugh combined.

'Rollo likes you!' Layla said.

Tio smiled and then said again, 'I'll be all right . . . Let us tell you about Ana.'

'She started singing!' Layla exclaimed.

'Just as the monoctohog was about to hit her. And then it stopped – just when it was this far away from reaching her. Just as she started to sing.' Tio held out two of his fingers in a small pinch to show how close the tentacle had come to me.

'You stopped it by singing?' Dodo asked, her eyes shining.

'I don't know why I did it,' I said. 'I don't know why it stopped, either.'

'Maybe it was surprised,' Layla suggested.

'Or it wanted to listen more than it wanted to hurt you,' Tio said.

Dodo reached for my hand and squeezed it. 'I guess we'll never really know. But perhaps your singing made it realize how precious some things are.'

I felt a warm glow in my chest. It was the same feeling I'd had when I was singing. A sort of flowing power that connected me all the way from the tips of my fingers out to the world and to everything in it.

Dodo looked towards Tio again. 'Are you sure that you're okay?'

'I think I will be,' Tio said. He stretched out his legs a bit then gingerly took a few steps forward. 'I'm fine,' he said, surprised. 'I thought I'd hurt myself more than I had. But I think I'm okay.'

'That's good,' Dodo said. Layla looked a little puzzled and did her thinking-nose-scrunch face.

'Do you know where the other one has gone now – the one that threw you?' Dodo asked, looking around a little anxiously.

'It's gone, but we're not sure why. It seemed to speak to Rollo and then just left,' I said.

'Hmm,' Dodo said. 'I wonder what they spoke about.'

'You've been left in charge again, haven't you?' Layla said affectionately to Rollo. Rollo leaned towards Layla a little and she gently laid one of her hands onto one of its spines, but then she moved her hand away quickly as if she'd received a shock.

'It feels funny. Like there's an electrical current running through it, or something,' she explained.

Dodo crouched down close to Rollo.

'What are you?' she asked, reaching out for one of its spines too. Perhaps because she'd had Layla's warning, she was able to touch it for a little longer so didn't move her hand away in surprise.

She smiled at Layla and said, 'It feels really weird, doesn't it?'

Rollo extended one of its tentacles towards Dodo's opening hand. Very slowly, Rollo touched its tentacle to her palm.

Rollo remained very still, but I noticed how its spines flickered and stood up a little taller. It was as though it had learned something new. Then I saw one of its tentacles slowly starting to unfurl. It was reaching towards Dodo's pocket as if it was looking for something, but more than that, I could tell by the way it was moving that it knew what was in her pocket.

I thought about all the pictures Rollo had been hiding, and how Layla said it had felt so funny to touch, and what Dodo had written in her note, and suddenly I remembered something: Dodo's note had said she was hiding something – but what?

'You've got the camera recording on you, haven't you?' I asked. 'That was the thing that you wanted to hide here.'

Dodo's hand broke contact with Rollo and she stuck it into her pocket, the one that Rollo's tentacle was reaching for. She pulled out a dull silver memory stick.

'Is that the only copy?' I asked.

'Yes,' Dodo said.

'Rollo knows about that, somehow. I think it knew you had it in your pocket, just then. After it touched your hand, it started to go towards your pocket.'

'Maybe it can read all her memories through touch,' Tio said in a burst and then followed up with, 'or maybe that sounds ridiculous.'

'No, I think you're right – it is something like that,' I said.

'I think its touch can do something else, too,' Layla said to Tio. 'You weren't able to move before – it's only since Rollo touched you that you started to feel better. Before that you were seriously injured.'

'You think Rollo healed me,' Tio said in a questioning, unbelieving kind of way.

'I don't know, but you fell so badly and you weren't able to move at all.'

I nodded, remembering the empty, dull sound Tio's body had made as he'd hit the ground.

Dodo looked from us back to Rollo.

'If they were responsible for making everyone stay asleep, then I imagine they have all kinds of powers that we can't really imagine,' she said. She held the memory stick in front of Rollo. 'So, you know about this too?'

'The other monoctohog touched you when we arrived. That was when it wanted to try to take you away. When they were talking, maybe Rollo convinced it that we would give them the memory stick. Maybe it's all part of the experiment. I think we need to give it to Rollo – or destroy it. And maybe, when we do that, this will all be over,' I said.

'We'll lose our memory of today?' Layla said.

'And wake up like it's just a normal day and everyone else will be awake too?' Tio added.

'I don't know, but we could give it a go,' I said.

'It's definitely worth a try,' Dodo said. She held out the memory stick towards Rollo, but then she quickly withdrew her hand and tucked the stick back into her fist.

'What is it?' Layla asked.

'I just want to look at it for one more moment,' Dodo said. 'It really is the most extraordinary creature.'

Rollo's fur-scales rippled like a wave. The more I looked at the shiny darkness of them, the more colours I could see embedded into the black – it held the deepest reds, peacock blues and sunny yellows.

'Okay,' Dodo said, and she finally presented the memory stick to Rollo.

'Wait!' Tio suddenly shouted.

'What is it?' I asked.

'Do you really think we're not going to remember anything? What if Rollo puts us back to sleep when it has that memory stick? Will we wake up like it's just a normal day again?' Tio asked.

'I don't know, but we probably won't remember,' I said.

Tio's face was difficult to read. His eyes held mine for a long time and then he looked away.

'Well, maybe we'll be able to remember little bits,' Layla said. 'Like Dodo with her drawings.'

'But we won't be able to make sense of them,' I said. 'Just like she couldn't.'

'So we'll stop talking again,' Tio said.

'I guess so,' I said.

'Maybe we'll be able to remember – if we all really, really

want to?' Layla said. 'Like how we woke Dodo up. We've seen how powerful we can be when we unite.'

'I think you'll remember,' Dodo said quietly. 'If you really want to.'

Tio gave a tiny nod. I looked over to his face – there was Tio, my old friend, and mixed up with it, the face of the person who'd tormented me and made me feel so small. I realized that I'd been making them different in my head – almost as if they were two separate people – but of course that was not true. And when we woke up again, with our altered memories, it'd go back to how it was before. The Tio who hated me. I wouldn't be able to understand why he was behaving so badly and reach out to him, and he would just think I'd chosen Layla over him. But they were the same person; I realized that now. The reason why he was being so horrible was because he wanted to be friends so much. It made no sense and all the sense at the same time.

'I think we'll remember too. The people we really are.' Tio smiled over at me and I tried to freeze his face in my mind. How his smile was a bit lopsided and one of his front teeth jutted out ever so slightly. How in that moment his eyes looked like all the universe was in them – stars, planets and black holes. I tried to preserve the picture in my mind.

'Shall I give it to Rollo?' Dodo asked gently.

'Hold on,' I said. I reached out a hand each to Tio and to Layla. Their palms connected with mine and though I knew I was imagining it, it felt like a heartbeat, steady and sure, ran through us all.

Dodo handed the memory stick to Rollo who picked it up delicately and, once again, tucked it away into an imperceptible gap amid the close pattern of its spines.

'You know, we might have got this wrong completely,' Layla said. 'And nothing might happen at all.'

But then three of Rollo's tentacles reached out to us. The one coming towards me connected to my chest.

It felt like a shot of something, an injection of a good sensation. It was kindness, curiosity and relief, all wrapped up together. It jolted through my body and made me feel unable to speak. And at the same time, I could feel waves of sleep start to come over me.

Like a snowstorm in reverse, I sensed parts of today had already started to float away from me.

'Don't forget,' I heard Tio murmur next to me. I wasn't even sure if we were still standing at this point, we were so lost in the waves of this feeling that was taking us away. I tried to open my eyes, but the lids were glued shut – it was impossible to keep them open.

Then I heard Dodo beside me. She was muttering, half to herself, half to someone else, it seemed. But her words sank into my brain through the waves of sleep and I realized that she was speaking to me: 'Remember what you did. Remember you sang. You can do the things that you want to do even if you're scared you might not be good enough. That feeling, it doesn't matter. What matters is the trying, the exploring. You are going to be a great explorer. I know it, Ana Ban-ana.'

'An explorer? Like in other countries?' I muttered back drowsily. It took every effort to say the words and not sink into sleep. My mind filled with snow-capped mountains, red desert dunes and the tangled green of the rainforest from the pictures on Dodo's bedroom wall.

'There's more than one kind of explorer.' Her voice had

dropped quieter than a whisper now. Her breath fell heavily and I almost didn't make out her last words before I went under. 'Just keep ... keep going, keep growing.'

Then I just heard her breath, or perhaps my breath, and I felt like I was going down the slide of a helter-skelter, round and round, faster and faster and faster until I knew that ...

I was fast asleep.

CASE #41029973876628

Case Holder Notes:

WEDNESDAY – 6.57 p.m.

Case concluded.

Personal Note by Case Holder: Due to multiple breaches, Case Holder faces disciplinary action and possible re-allocation, but Case Holder has seen extraordinary things and will never forget the unifying behaviours of Primary Subject + Companion Subject + Girl #3.

Initiate clear-up.

WEDNESDAY (AGAIN)

7.30 a.m.

It takes a big effort to open my eyes. I blink once, twice, then clench my fingers into a fist and rub at my face. I stretch for a moment, enjoying the elasticity of my muscles but I'm lying on something hard that digs into my back so I sit up.

I'm wearing my school uniform.

My rucksack is on my back – that's the bumpy thing beneath me.

I pull on the sleeve of my jumper and stare at it through sleep-filled eyes, but it doesn't change the fact that I have no idea why I'm wearing it. *I must have put it on in my sleep*, I think, although that idea niggles me and I have no memory of getting dressed.

I look outside my bedroom window, and see that the sky is patched over with greyish clouds. The light is thin.

Suddenly, my head fills with a dream I just had, but it only comes back to me in bits and pieces that feel impossible to stitch together. My head swims from remembering something. A kind of creature that moves like a monkey but looks like an octopus. It was a weird dream, the type that feels so vividly real, but also so strange that it can't have possibly happened. And then, oddly, I think of Tio. Tio from next door. The last thing I can remember about him is how he laughed at me in the school hall, but I have the niggling urge to go and see him. I can't explain why. The other odd thing is that I don't feel anxious about seeing him. I have a feeling of excitement and anticipation as if I'm waking up on my birthday.

Without thinking, I jump out of bed and rush through the living room.

'Morning, pops.' I spin round to see Mum hunched over her pile of books. 'You're ready nice and early.'

I freeze for a moment. There's nothing out of the ordinary about Mum sitting at the table, but something about it makes me stop.

'Are you okay?' I hear myself asking.

'Yes, fine, fine,' Mum says. 'And don't worry about Dodo, okay? I got a message from her early this morning saying she was all right.'

'Dodo,' I murmur, remembering all that had happened the night before with her forgetting Chewy Tuesdays and the weird videocall she made.

'I just need to check something,' I say to Mum as I wrench open the front door.

'Where are you going?' Mum calls behind me.

'Nowhere,' I call back. I've no idea why I need to look out in the corridor, but I know that I must.

For a moment the corridor is silent, but then sounds from next door burst into the space as a front door swings open. Tio appears on the other side of it. He glances up and down the corridor and then he locks eyes with me.

'Morning,' he says.

'Morning,' I say back. I have the weirdest feeling, like

something has changed between us, even though I have no idea what it is. Tio looks as surprised as I feel.

'See you later,' I blurt out and then shut my front door, but not before I hear him saying the same back to me. There's a gentleness in his tone that I've not heard in months and months. Not since Layla joined our class, at the end of last year. I can almost picture the moment as clearly as though it was happening right then and there. We'd just been told to sit down at our desks and Tio had said 'see you later', just like he'd done now. The door of our classroom had opened and Layla came in. It surprises me that I'm able to remember this, but there it is, clear as day.

'Who was that?' Mum asks.

'Tio,' I say.

'Everything all right between you two?' Mum asks.

'Umm . . . yes,' I say, trying to avoid her glare.

'I know that . . .' Mum starts to say, 'there's been some issues. I wanted to talk to you about it last night, but everything with Dodo took over. I spoke to Benny about it yesterday.'

I open my mouth to protest, but something stops me. Instead, I just tell her the truth. 'He's been mean to me for a while now.'

'Oh, pops,' Mum says. 'I'm sorry. What's been happening?'

'It's just little things – laughing at me, teasing me, that kind of thing. It's been . . . a bit horrible.'

The room somehow feels a little brighter now I've told Mum about it. Sunlight suddenly streams through the window, and in its rays I can see particles of dust dancing in the light. A weight shifts from my shoulders. I'm standing taller. It feels good to stand like that.

'Benny mentioned that Tio's been feeling pushed out by you and Layla, a little,' Mum says slowly.

211

I open my mouth to protest, but before I can get any words out, a wave of understanding rushes over me.

'It might have started when Layla joined actually,' I say, thinking more about Layla's first day at school. 'So, Tio thinks I don't want to be friends with him any more?'

'I know friendships can get complicated,' Mum says. 'And I'm not excusing Tio's behaviour. I just wonder if there's a way you two can make up.'

'Maybe,' I said. 'I used to think not, but maybe there is.'

I'm surprised as I say those words. I can't fully explain where they've come from. Yesterday, I felt so sure that I never wanted to speak to Tio again but today, though only a night's sleep has passed, I have the feeling of possibility. Possibility that maybe things could be okay, after all.

WEDNESDAY (AGAIN)

8.31 a.m.

I run towards school to make it in time to meet Layla at her mum's flat. I want to get there before she leaves.

As I knock on the door, I'm met almost immediately by Layla's startled face.

'What are—?'

'I'm sorry about yesterday,' I say quickly.

'It's okay,' she says after a moment. I feel myself uncoil.

'I didn't mean to act like that,' I say. 'I was just – embarrassed, I guess.'

'It's okay, I understand. I should have listened to you when you said you didn't want me to make a big deal out of it.'

'No,' I say, reaching for her hand. 'I'm glad that you did. It's who you are.'

'It's funny. I think I dreamed about you,' she says.

'You know, now you say that, I think you were in my dream, too.' I pause.

'There was something else,' Layla says, scrunching her hand against her hair, trying to remember. 'No, it's gone.'

She looks towards one of the bushes outside her house.

'What is it?' I ask.

'Nothing. I don't know. I thought I saw something but there's nothing there.'

I look over to the bushes. Their emerald leaves are speckled with yellow and hang silent and still. I have that funny sensation when you can't quite remember what was a dream and what was real. The longer I look at the bush, the more the feeling grows.

'It's all right to fall out, you know,' Layla says, interrupting my thoughts. 'What's more important is making up.'

I nod and pull my gaze away from the bushes, although something still nags at me, but I'm not sure what exactly.

'Yes, I think you're right about that – the most important thing is making up,' I say, and as I speak, Tio floats into my mind and settles there. It's almost as if he's there with us, his kind, bright eyes meeting mine, and I realize that the odd feeling I'm holding inside is one of missing him.

'What is it?' Layla asks because I've gone quiet.

'It's weird,' I say. 'I was thinking of Tio. Mum says she spoke to his mum and she thinks he's been so mean to me because he's felt like we pushed him out.'

Layla looks like she's going to answer straight away but then considers what I've said and falls quiet.

'That's odd, but it could be the truth,' she says.

'It's weird but today I feel like everything could be different. Yesterday, I felt so ... so stuck, like things wouldn't ever change or get any better. And nothing's really changed, but today I feel like maybe I might even be able to talk to Tio again.'

'I guess stranger things have happened,' Layla replies.

'What did you say?' I ask.

'Stranger things have happened,' Layla repeats.

'Didn't you say something about that before?' I ask.

'What do you mean?' Layla replies, looking confused.

'I don't know. I just had the oddest sense of déjà vu of you saying something about stranger things happening.'

Layla looks out to the road behind me as a bus rolls by and a mum with a buggy wanders past.

'I don't know – it seems like the same old world out there today,' she says.

WEDNESDAY (AGAIN)

1.43 p.m.

'So, any takers for the solo?' Ms Randall asks.

It's been a normal kind of morning with assembly, literacy and maths. I haven't seen Tio very much, or even spoken to him since I saw him in the corridor earlier, but I've felt him looking at me every now and then. It wasn't in an unkind way, though; it was more like he was trying to get my attention.

After lunch, Ms Randall said we needed to make some decisions about the Stars Concert. She showed us the song lyrics again, and then started asking us some questions about how we'd like to organize things.

Now she looks across the classroom, her question still hanging in the air. No one puts up their hand.

'I'd like to try,' I say, raising my hand quickly. It's weird – I feel as though I put my hand up before I'd even thought about doing it.

'Ana, that's great.'

I think some people might be looking over at me, but I keep my gaze focused and give Ms Randall a little nod.

Then someone else raises their hand. It takes me a moment to realize that it's Tio.

'Could I do some percussion for the song?' he asks.

'Well, I hadn't thought of that, but I can't see why not as long as it all sounds good during the rehearsals. That'd be brilliant, Tio. Thank you.'

I look over at Tio and he smiles back at me. It's a real smile, like in the corridor this morning. He seems surprised at himself.

'Let's get started now,' says Ms Randall, but as she clicks on her computer, the screen freezes and it makes an error noise. 'I'm going to have to restart it,' she says. 'Just chat among yourselves for a moment, please.'

Layla dips her head towards mine. 'You're going to be so great at the concert.'

'I'm going to give it a try,' I say. 'What's the worst that could happen – that I sound like the cat yowling from the playground and everybody hates it? They'll get over it.'

Layla laughs. It sounds like daisies. Today, everything that happened yesterday – Tio hearing me sing and the whole class finding out that Layla had never actually heard me sing – doesn't seem to matter that much for some reason. I think about how a single day can make you see things in a new way. Yesterday it all felt too much, and I was overwhelmed by feeling upset about what had happened with Tio and thinking that I was never going to sing again. But today, I can take it in my stride. I prefer feeling this way. I like thinking that I can try my best and that I don't have to worry about what other people think.

A few people overhear me and they laugh along with Layla.

I look over at Tio, who's chatting to Della, but I can see he's looking over towards me and Layla. I think back to Mum telling me about her conversation with Benny. If what Mum told me is really true, it means Tio thinks I've been ignoring him.

He's sitting too far away to speak to, but I do a little mime of

217

drumming and then give him a thumbs up. I feel a bit silly as I do it, and part of me wonders if he'll just look away, but he gives me a thumbs up back and the same smile again. It's his real smile, the one I haven't seen for months.

Ms Randall moves on and starts the lesson, and all the while a little light inside me begins to glow.

WEDNESDAY (AGAIN)

4.40 p.m.

'I'm fine. Honestly, I'm fine,' Dodo says, even though she's lying in a hospital bed.

Mum purses her lips. 'Let's just get you checked over, shall we?'

Mum came to collect me straight from school and we rushed to meet Dodo at the hospital.

'It's just not worth the risk, Doe,' she says now. 'Best to be sure.'

Mum went to see Dodo while I was at school because she was still concerned about the chunk of Monday evening that she couldn't remember. So Mum took her to the hospital to get more tests. Though I know Mum is worried, Dodo looks bright and cheerful.

'Your mum!' Dodo says. 'She's such a worrywart.'

'I'm going to go buy us some sandwiches so we can have dinner with you before visiting hours are over,' Mum says, ignoring Dodo. 'I won't be long.'

She kisses me on the head before she leaves.

'You know I was only teasing her,' Dodo says. 'She's right that I should get this checked out. It's the weirdest feeling to have gaps in my memory. But I do think I'm okay.'

'What's the last thing you remember now?' I ask.

'Well, it's strange,' Dodo says. 'I guess I was at the railway checking on the fox family camera. I'm not sure why I went back because I was only there a few days ago. But then I got home and went to sleep. I had some really vivid dreams. I dreamed I was back there, at the railway, and you were there, too.'

'Me?'

'Yes, with your best friends.'

'Layla?'

'Yes, and Tio.'

'Tio's not my best friend any more,' I say. 'But I'm trying to make up with him.' It all floods back to me now. I remember I was going to ask Dodo what she thought about Tio and what I should do. But after today, it doesn't seem like such a big problem any more.

'Well, in my dream he was one of your best friends. It was the three of you: Layla, Tio and you.'

'Then it was definitely a dream,' I say, laughing. 'Not a memory you've lost.'

Dodo rests one of her hands gently against her forehead.

'Right. It all seemed so real. Anyway, tell me about your day.'

'I decided to sing a solo at the concert,' I tell her.

'Oh, Ana, that's brilliant. You'll be brilliant.' Her face lights up and she leans forward on the bed, suddenly looking so well that it seems so wrong for her to be stuck in hospital.

I stare down at my shoes, but mutter a thank you.

A memory springs to my mind, although it's fuzzy round the edges.

'Didn't we talk about this already?' I ask, confused. 'But we couldn't have because it only happened today and we didn't chat about it last night. I think I remember us talking about singing recently?'

'I don't know,' Dodo says, shrugging her shoulders. 'I'm the worst person to ask about memories right now. What do you think I said?'

'Something about not giving up, about trying to do things you love even when you're scared of them.'

'That sounds like something it would be good to remember,' Dodo says.

'I won't forget,' I say. 'I promise I won't.'

Dodo lies back in her bed and looks towards the window next to her.

'Could you open up those blinds, please?' she asks me. 'At least I can have a good view while I'm here.'

I pull up the blinds and stand there for a moment. From the window, we can see the lights of the city in the distance – they look beautiful. The buildings and the skyline fit together like a perfectly finished puzzle. Among them, I can see the movement of people: the cars and buses on the road, the flicker of lights in homes. But because it's starting to get dark, we can also see the reflection of the two of us in the window.

For a moment, pulling the curtains back makes me think of what it might be like to be on stage when the curtains open for the Stars Concert. There aren't any actual curtains on our school stage, but the thought fills me with excitement nonetheless. In just a few weeks' time, I'll stand on that stage and sing. I never thought I'd be able to do that. I didn't think I was good enough and I was worried what people would think of me. I remind myself how I've been feeling that way more and more recently. But now I can imagine Mum and Dodo in the crowd, and Layla, and even Tio there, urging me on. It feels like things between us will be all right after all. Warmth floods through me.

I say it to myself one more time: *In a couple of weeks' time, I will stand up and sing.*

I straighten my back. I stand tall.

A TRANSCRIPT OF THE DISCIPLINARY HEARING FOR THE CASE HOLDER OF CASE #41029973876628

SPEAKER: Thank you to all on the Panel for attending this disciplinary hearing for the Case Holder of Case #41029973876628. I will be your Speaker for the duration.

First of all, can I please check that you have read and understood the following reports:

Case Holder Notes #41029973876628
Case Supervisor Testimony #41029973876628
Error Report #41029973876628 #1: Primary Subject Relative
Error Report #41029973876628 #2: Primary Subject + Companion Subject
Error Report #41029973876628 #3: Primary Subject + Companion Subject
Proximity Alert #41029973876628 #1: Subject Wipe (Partial Success) of Primary Subject Relative
Proximity Alert #41029973876628 #2: Defensive Shield: Level Two of Primary Subject and Companion Subject
Proximity Alert #41029973876628 #3: Defensive Shield: Level Seven of Primary Subject and Companion Subject
Connection Report #41029973876628 #1: Primary Subject =

Companion Subject
Connection Report #41029973876628 #2: Primary Subject +
Companion Subject = Girl #3
Connection Report #41029973876628 #3: Primary Subject +
Companion Subject + Girl #3 = Primary Subject Relative.

PANEL: The reports have been read and understood.

SPEAKER: Thank you. As you are aware, though this is
a relatively new project, our Case Work has proved very
successful across multiple universes in our quest to understand
the behaviour of different dominant planetary species, without
drawing attention to our presence.

Using our technologies, a Primary Subject who pres-
ents with High Energy Tension is chosen at random and a
Companion Subject is selected who interacts with the Primary
Subject with a Low Energy Connection. Their Energy Tension
and Connection is monitored for one planetary day, while
all other members of their species and their dependants are
placed in a rest state. We wipe memories of the day for the
Subjects once the Case is terminated.

This disciplinary hearing has been called to address
the multiple breaches of Regulation 1.1928 in Case
#41029973876628.

Regulation 1.1928 refers to when a Case Holder pur-
posefully, and knowingly, reveals themself to a Primary
Subject or Companion Subject. We are also here to consider
the numerous Error Reports and Proximity Alerts in this Case.

I would firstly like to draw your attention to the Case
Holder's inexperience in Case Work. This was the Case

Holder's first Case. However, this Case has a much higher number of regulation breaches, Error Reports and Proximity Alerts than we hold on record for any Case Holder's initial Case.

It was nothing more than an unfortunate coincidence that the Case Holder encountered a relative of the Primary Subject on arrival at the Transport Base, detailed in Error Report #41029973876628 #1 and Proximity Alert #41029973876628 #1: Subject Wipe (Partial Success) of Primary Subject Relative.

The fact that the memory wipe of Primary Subject Relative was not fully successful was indeed down to a lack of experience. Fortunately, the Case Holder's technique for the memory wipes of the Subjects and Girl #3 showed great improvement and these memory wipes were successful.

I would also like to draw your attention to some other unusual factors in this Case. The number of Connection Reports is much higher than average, too.

Firstly, the Primary Subject was able to rouse the Companion Subject from a rest state during the planetary day. A Companion Subject may enter a rest state if the Subjects separate and a Low Energy Connection continues. In such circumstances, should the Companion Subject remain in a rest state, the Case would be terminated.

However, not only did the Primary Subject wake the Companion Subject due to the strength of their Energy Connection, but the Primary Subject and Companion Subject also made an Energy Connection so great that together they woke Girl #3 from a rest state.

The Primary Subject, Companion Subject and Girl #3 made

a further Energy Connection together in order to cross the Defensive Shield at Level Five, which is when the Case Holder made the first breach of Regulation 1.1928.

The Defensive Shield can only be employed if the Subjects, or any member of the dominant species of the test planet, approaches the Transport Base, triggering a Proximity Alert. It is at the discretion of the Case Holder to decide at what level the Defensive Shield is set, once a Proximity Alert is triggered. The Defensive Shield at Level Two would produce an effect of moderate nausea alongside moderate flu-like symptoms. The Defensive Shield at Level Seven would produce an effect of extreme nausea alongside extreme flu-like symptoms, rendering the Subject unable to progress. Therefore, the Energy Connection that the Primary Subject, Companion Subject and Girl #3 made should be considered alongside the high level of the Defensive Shield.

Finally, the Primary Subject, Companion Subject and Girl #3 woke Primary Subject Relative from rest state by making another significant Energy Connection.

Another unusual aspect of Case #41029973876628 is that the Case Supervisor gave consent for the Case to continue despite the multiple breaches of Regulation 1.1928, Error Reports and Proximity Alerts. This was due to the Case Supervisor's witnessing the Primary Subject's act of 'singing'.

The Energy Tension and Connection Shifts in this Case are indeed highly unusual, and as you see they are described in the Case Holder Notes as 'extraordinary'.

Having reviewed the reports and my outline of the Case as your Speaker, what do you, the Panel, recommend?

PANEL: The Case Holder's inexperience shows throughout this Case, particularly in the execution of an only partially successful memory wipe on a human who was related to the Primary Subject.

Nevertheless, we do not see that the inexperience of the Case Holder was a reasonable explanation for the high number of Error Reports and Proximity Alerts alongside the multiple breaches of Regulation 1.1928.

We recognize that the Connection Reports in this Case are unlike any we hold on record for past Cases on Planet #555535468979897875765.

The reports do show a highly unusual Energy Tension Shift in the Case Supervisor, and also the Primary Subject, at the moment of 'singing' by the Primary Subject.

Our recommendation is that the Case Holder be removed from Case Work indefinitely. We do not advise any further disciplinary action.

SPEAKER: This concludes this disciplinary hearing. Once more, thank you to the Panel for attending.
The Case Holder will be notified of the Panel's judgement.

HEARING CONCLUDED.

ACKNOWLEDGEMENTS

Hugest thanks to two superstars: my agent, Clare Wallace, and my editor, Amina Youssef. I keep telling you both that I couldn't do this without you. So now I'll write it here for good measure. Thank you always for the whole-hearted support and care.

I'm so thrilled to be working with the brilliant team at Simon & Schuster Children's Books, whose tireless passion and energy have brought *The Day No One Woke Up* and such an incredible list of books into readers' hands. Thank you, Rachel Denwood, Ali Dougal, David McDougall, Sean Williams, Eve Wersocki Morris, Olivia Horrox, Laura Hough, Dani Wilson, Sophie Storr, Jane Pizzey, Dominic Brendon, Anna Bowles and Leena Lane.

A big shout out to the fabulous Darley Anderson Literary Agency crew: Mary Darby, Lydia Silver, Kristina Egan, Georgia Fuller, Sheila David, Rosanna Bellingham and Chloe Davis. You move mountains! Thank you, always.

Thank you to George Ermos for creating a truly stunning cover.

And, finally, thanks to Dan and B. Thank you for continuing to entertain me and encourage my stories. More, different books!

About the author

Polly Ho-Yen used to be a primary school teacher in London. While she was teaching, she used to get up very early in the morning to write stories. The first of those stories became her critically acclaimed debut novel *Boy in the Tower*, which was shortlisted for the Waterstones Children's Book Prize and the Blue Peter Book Award. She lives in Bristol with her husband and daughter.

Don't miss out on reading
another brilliant book by

POLLY HO-YEN

'A FABULOUS PAGE-TURNER'
ABI ELPHINSTONE, AUTHOR OF *SKY SONG*

How I
SAVED
The
WORLD
in a
WEEK

POLLY HO-YEN

Illustrations by George Ermos

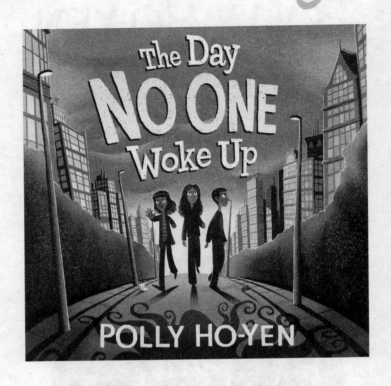

is also available to listen
to as an audiobook!